WILD
BEAUTIFUL
PLACES

WILD
BEAUTIFUL
PLACES

Picture-Perfect Journeys Around the Globe

Foreword by George W. Stone, Editor in Chief,
National Geographic Traveler magazine

NATIONAL GEOGRAPHIC

CONTENTS

One of nature's many moods in the brooding Superstition Mountains of Arizona, United States (page I); the serene Lake of the Woods, Ontario, Canada (pages 2–3); and a giant's bed of nails, the limestone pinnacles of western Madagascar (left).

Unspoiled Beauty

You are holding one of National Geographic's most audacious books. Embedded in our mission of "inspiring people to care about the planet" is the notion that inspiration comes from knowledge. But what about inspiration that comes from awe? From the visceral, immediate, and unfiltered power of experiencing such elemental, untrammeled wilderness that human response is reduced to a babbling brook?

Now that's wild. And that's our starting point. Our appreciation of beauty is rooted in vulnerability: first our willingness to expose ourselves to the natural world as it is; then to consider that, because of our presence, the natural world is more vulnerable than it might otherwise be. At the heart of *Wild, Beautiful Places* is an acknowledgment that we need Brazil's Pantanal, Hawaii's Molokai Cliffs, and Antarctica's Weddell Sea more than these places need us. Namibia's Skeleton Coast is so called precisely for its power to cut human encroachment to the bone.

And yet wild places do need us today, and perhaps in exchange they offer us the gift of self-discovery and inspire within us a sense of purpose. When a young Teddy Roosevelt first traveled to the Dakota Territory in 1883, it was to hunt bison; his exposure to the wild fueled his passion as a conservationist. When he established Montana's National Bison Range in 1908 (marking the first time that U.S. tax dollars were used to preserve wildlife), it was an expression not only of his philosophical transformation through travel, but also of his personal sense of ecological connectedness and obligation in the world. Roosevelt saw that the preservation of the nation's wildlife, no matter how far-flung, should become an emblem of national identity and a reminder that an industrial power remained wild at heart.

In wildness we discover ourselves. These 50 journeys show that our choice to travel to Tasmania, Bhutan, and Chile's Tierra del Fuego can be seen as daring personal efforts to experience the world at its core. But the important discovery is that when we ascribe beauty to wild places, we reveal more about our own values than about the world. And so if we listen to ourselves, to the words we use to describe our wilderness, and to the photos that showcase it, we may find that we have all the inspiration we need to preserve the wild for generations to come.

—George W. Stone

Editor in Chief, *National Geographic Traveler*

The roseate spoonbill *(Ajaja ajaja)* is known for its pink plumage and flattened beak, and feeds in shallow coastal waters of the southern United States and South America.

The undulating
shoreline of Molokai,
Hawaii, United States

Two figures dwarfed
by snow-laden trees
in the Swiss Alps

It's a new day at
Canyonlands National Park,
Utah, United States

North America

Yawning chasms, towering mountains, soaring sea cliffs, and iceberg-choked fjords: North America has big landscapes—and seascapes.

Nahanni National Park

Nahanni National Park Reserve is renowned for the formidable peaks of the Cirque of the Unclimbables, but the landscape is more than the sum of its spires and plateaus. It is also a cultural tapestry of the region, one where history is threaded through the land, from gold rush tales of murder and revenge, to the legends of the Dehcho First Nations people who have inhabited it for millennia.

Because of its remote location on the Continental Divide separating Yukon from the Northwest Territories, Nahanni sees far fewer tourists than most of Canada's national parks—in 2015, it had only 1,016 visitors, most via floatplane. There are no public roads inside Nahanni, and the few overland routes that access the park are very rugged. The plane trip from Fort Simpson, a community with a population of around 1,200, takes an average of 90 minutes. Time passes quickly, however, when you're staring out the window at the Mackenzie River—Canada's longest—winding through vast tundra on its way to the Arctic Ocean.

Nahanni comprises more than 11,583 square miles (30,000 sq km) of harsh and diverse wilderness—this includes mountains that reach 8,661 feet (2,640 m), ice fields, tundra, boreal forest, and incredible karst formations that are a Swiss cheese of sinkholes and caves. Within this region are 180 species of birds and 42 species of mammals including trumpeter swans, grizzly bears, black bears, moose, and the Nahanni Complex, the name given to the three caribou herds in the park.

The northern mountain caribou (above) live in the rugged Mackenzie Mountains of Canada's Northwest Territories, an area partially protected within the spiny ridges and shadowy valleys of the vast Nahanni National Park Reserve (opposite).

The South Nahanni River
cuts its way through four
deep canyons.

From Fort Simpson, Nahanni has only seven designated landing spaces for floatplanes. These include Glacier Lake, the most popular entry point for visiting the Cirque of the Unclimbables, a ring of dramatic granite peaks in the Mackenzie Mountain Range polished slick and weathered into sheer pinnacles by centuries of wind and snow.

Despite their name and foreboding appearance, adventurers with considerable technical skill regularly climb the ragged spires. One of the most popular routes is the climb up the beautiful, vertical stone-fluted Lotus Flower Tower. It's a long slog from Glacier Lake to the lush alpine meadows at the base of the Tower, and the ascent to the 8,440-foot (2,573 m) peak can take more than a full day—but the 360-degree views from the top are awesome.

Another popular landing site for floatplanes is Virginia Falls, known in Dene as Náįlįcho, meaning "big river falling." Here the South Nahanni River thunders over a ledge that rises more than 3,000 feet (914 m) above the Painted Canyon below—a cascade twice the height of Niagara Falls.

There are less expected geological wonders too. At Rabbitkettle Lake, natural hot springs bubble from beneath the earth. A short hike from the lake takes you out to Nahanni's famous tufa mounds, a series of terraces—some believed to be 10,000 years old—created by years of salt-laden groundwater evaporating and leaving behind hardened calcium carbonate. In Dene legend, one of these mounds is home to Yamoria, "protector of the people." This spirit is said to have gone down to the confluence of the Liard and

Sure-footed and steady, Dall sheep pluck their way
up the Backbone Ranges of the Mackenzie Mountains.

South Nahanni Rivers to drive away giant beavers that drowned boaters by slapping their massive tails to upset the canoes.

Elsewhere in the park, grim monikers like the Funeral Range, Headless Creek, and Deadmen Valley might seem to caution visitors contemplating an excursion into Nahanni. Actually, these names are a legacy of the region's gold prospecting history. During and after the Klondike gold rush, prospectors used the Nahanni region to access the storied Yukon gold fields. Details are hazy, but some of these prospectors turned up dead and headless in the early 20th century, a morbid circumstance reflected in the park's place-names.

REWIND AN OUTPOST SCHOOL

National Geographic photographer and explorer Amos Burg spent the summer of 1929 paddling 1,800 miles (2,900 km) through northern Canada, partially retracing the steps of North American trailblazer Alexander Mackenzie, who had navigated Canada's northern river systems all the way to the Arctic Ocean in 1789 (the Mackenzie River is named for him).

Provisioned with three months' worth of bacon and hardtack, Burg faced his own hardships. He almost rowed his canoe over a 20-foot (6.7 m) drop ("Only the plucky paddling of my companions saved us from being dashed to the bottom of the falls"); he was constantly besieged by mosquitoes ("Meals were an ordeal for each bite of bacon was punished by six bites from the mosquitoes"); and a bad knee caused him agony. In the Mackenzie district of the Northwest Territories, Burg stopped off at the school in the remote hamlet of Fort McPherson and met John Morris (pictured), an Anglican missionary and teacher to Peel and Loucheux tribal children.

Dehcho First Nations people have been instrumental in managing Nahanni, or Naha Dehé (meaning "river of the mountain people") since it was established in 1976 as a reserve, and now are part of a consensus team that co-manages it with Parks Canada. A visit during July or August means guests can connect with the park's staff, many of whom are First Nations and can interpret the stories behind the landscape.

▶ TRAVELWISE

• **HOW TO VISIT** A chartered floatplane will bring you into the park from Fort Simpson. Weather in the Cirque is unpredictable. Spring means flooding, so best to wait until June to travel, but be flexible. Storms can crop up midday, stalling flights or climbing expeditions.

• **PLANNING** Information about the park is at the Parks Canada site (*pc.gc.ca/eng/pn-np/nt/nahanni/index.aspx*). Outfitters run multiday canoe trips and rafting excursions (try Black Feather at *nahanniriver.ca*).

• **HOW TO STAY** The entire park is open to dispersed camping (visit the park website to check area closures), and Parks Canada also runs a campground. Fort Simpson has a number of inns and hotels.

PICTURE PERFECT

The world's best alpinists call Cirque of the Unclimbables a pristine Yosemite Valley, tucked away in a remote corner of the Northwest Territories. Photographer Gordon Wiltsie was faced with the challenge of pinpointing the most dramatic but walkable ridge to capture the range's grandeur. "This one was perfect," he says, "with a narrow, flat top and cliffs falling away on either side." The next challenge? "Landing the helicopter. [It was] unlike any landing the pilot had ever done—though he thought we were the crazy ones!" Indeed, it's fairly certain no human had ever stood on—much less photographed—this incredible arête before.

IMAGE BY GORDON WILTSIE
National Geographic photographer

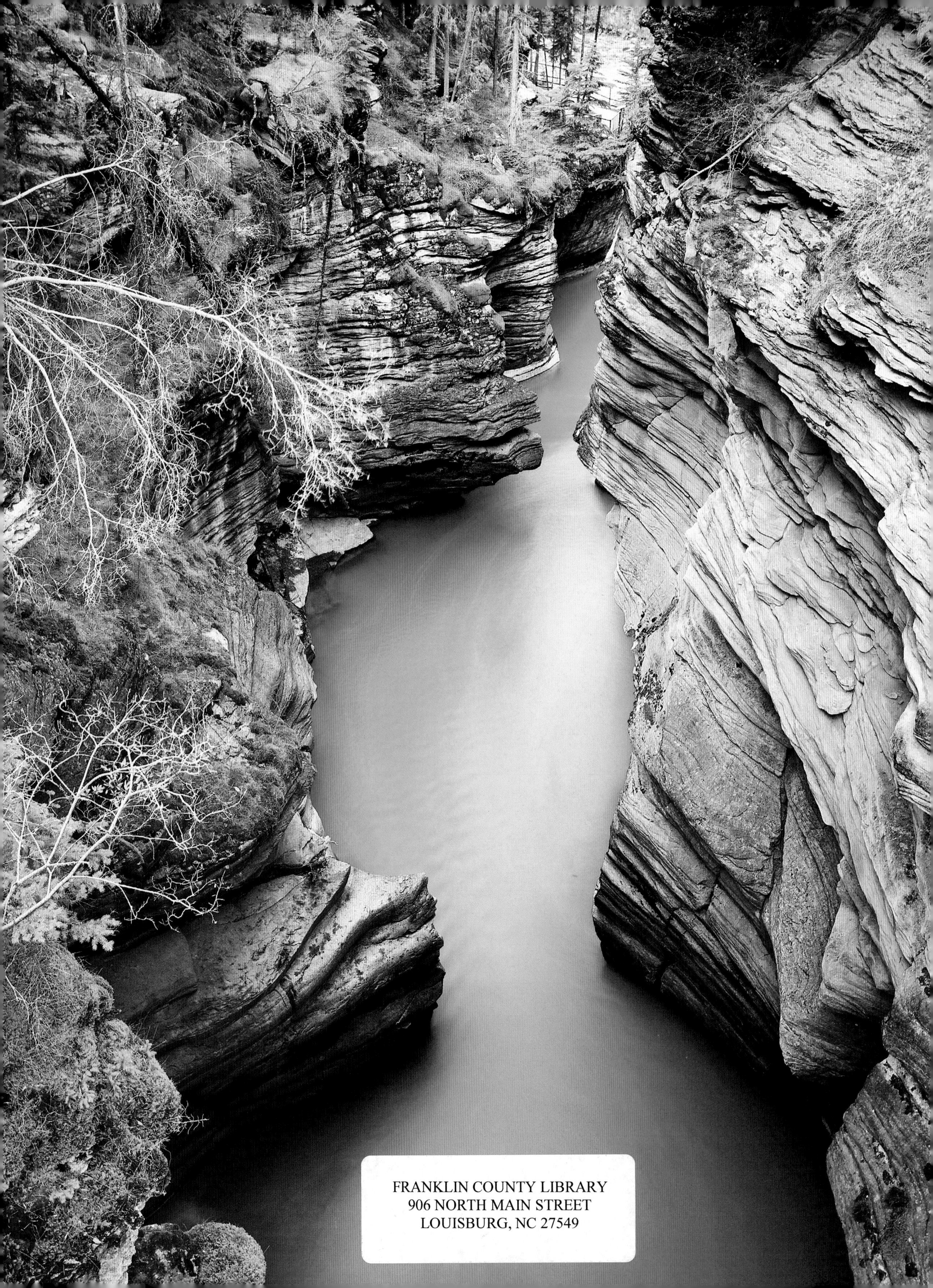

Jasper National Park

Some falls are known for their height; others for their power. The latter is true for Athabasca Falls in Jasper National Park, on the far western edge of Alberta. The water, roiling and cornflower blue, may only drop 75 feet (23 m), but it does so with such force and in such volume that the viewing platforms at the site are shrouded in a fine mist during the busy summer months.

The Athabasca River is an 870-mile (1,400 km) tributary that runs from the Columbia Icefield in the 4,335-square-mile (11,228 sq km) Jasper National Park through the Northwest Territories to the Arctic Ocean. In 1810, the British-Canadian cartographer and explorer David Thompson traveled the Athabasca looking for a fur trade route to the Pacific Ocean. His successful discovery of Athabasca Pass, which clears the Canadian Rockies at an elevation of roughly 5,750 feet (1,753 m), helped establish these routes.

Athabasca Falls are located in the middle of the river's run through the park. Here they flow over hard quartzite and softer limestone cliffs. Over the course of millennia, the torrent carved its way through this rock and formed a ragged, broadly stepped ledge over which the water cascades. It then courses through a narrow gorge below, frothing and hemmed in by wavy canyon walls. Mount Kerkeslin, a 9,800-foot (2,987 m) peak in the Canadian Rockies, looms over this entire spectacular site.

There's something to see at the falls, year-round. In September, male elk let out piercing bugles to summon females along the

Turquoise blue or streaming white, the mighty Athabasca River within Jasper National Park, Alberta, wears rock down into canyons (opposite) and stepped waterfalls (above).

Athabasca River; in the spring, elk calves are born. One of the most remarkable sights occurs in the winter, when temperatures in the park drop to an average maximum of 15°F (-9°C), and the fast-moving falls freeze into thick sheets of white and frosty blue icicles, suspended over the uneven stone ledges.

In summer, the park is a good place to hike. It boasts nearly 621 miles (1,000 km) of trails, including Sulphur Skyline. This 5-mile (8-km) hike promises stunning views of the remote and rugged Fiddle River Valley, the Miette Hot Springs, and Ashlar Ridge—a sheer, upright limestone cliff popular with rock climbers.

You'll find interesting ice caves and glacier formations at Mount Edith Cavell, not far from the falls. The Angel Glacier spills down the north face of the mountain and into a turquoise lake, its meltwater studded with icebergs. Hiking trails lead to ripple-walled ice caves within the glacier, though care should be taken when exploring this area. Falling rock, ice, and avalanches are not uncommon.

Meltwater carves a frothy stream into the Athabasca Glacier (opposite), which is protected by Jasper National Park. Specially designed vehicles ferry visitors onto the ice field.

> **TRAVELWISE**

• **HOW TO VISIT** The park is 192 miles (309 km) west of Edmonton, and accessible by Alberta Highway 93 from the south, and the Yellowhead Highway from the east and west. Bus shuttles are available from major Alberta airports to Jasper. VIA Rail (*viarail.ca*) and Greyhound also service the town.

• **PLANNING** The website operated by Parks Canada contains a variety of information on the park and falls (*pc.gc.ca/eng/pn-np/ab/jasper/index .aspx*), as does the Jasper National Park site (*jaspernationalpark.com*).

• **HOW TO STAY** Kerkeslin Campground is next to the Athabasca River. Less rustic accommodations in the town of Jasper include the Fairmont Jasper Park Lodge (*fairmont.com/jasper*) and a Hostelling International location (*hihostels.ca*).

Elk wade in the Athabasca River, where males bugle to attract females during mating season.

Molokai

Some say Molokai is what the Hawaiian Islands looked like 50 years ago; others would argue this is what the world should strive to resemble in the future. Untouched by mass development, this 10-mile-wide (16 km) island has over a hundred miles (161 km) of shoreline, hidden waterfalls, ancient ruins, and the proud native heritage of Hawaii. What it doesn't have? Even a single traffic light.

Molokai may be Hawaii's microcosm, a small island with varied climates that range from the arid west with secluded white sand beaches, to the verdant east where coconut palms, elephant ears, and banana plants grow in the lush Halawa Valley. The valley—with a history of human habitation dating back to the seventh century—ends with the pouring waters of the 250-foot (76 m) Moaula Falls and 500-foot (152 m) Hipuapua Falls.

Molokai's shoreline boasts the world's tallest sea cliffs, spectacular precipices that soar to heights of 3,900 feet (1,189 m). These giant coastal walls fringe Kalaupapa Peninsula on the island's remote northern coast, and only a hundred visitors daily are allowed to visit by aircraft or on foot—there is neither boat nor road access to the dramatic cliffs.

As idyllic as Kalaupapa Peninsula may appear now, the designated National Historical Park was once a desolate place, a quarantined leprosy colony for nearly a century from 1866. People afflicted by the disease were sentenced to permanent exile here; today, a handful of former patients continue to live here by choice.

The Hawaiian island of Molokai rises from the Pacific between Oahu and Maui. Here, nature is the main attraction: The island has serene beaches and the highest sea cliffs in the world (above and opposite).

The historic site is accessible on the back of mules (guided tour only) that pluck their way down the steep cliffs, giving visitors magnificent views out over the Pacific.

During the migration season from December through April, over 10,000 humpback whales glide through the waters surrounding the island. Miles of reef fringing Molokai contain dive sites where human visitors can commune with green sea turtles, dolphins, Hawaiian monk seals, and even manta rays. Summer, with sunny skies, is the best time to explore the coastline's coral beds and beaches.

Molokai's beauty also lies in its culture, which the locals proudly celebrate with folk festivals. With one of the highest concentrations of native Hawaiians in the archipelago, Molokai is touted as the birthplace of hula, the traditional Polynesian dance. The locals perform it at Makahiki, a Hawaiian New Year festival that takes place in towns across the island in honor of Lono, god of agriculture and fertility.

Molokai still has vast stretches of undeveloped landscape, with warm emerald waters (above) and sheer, crumpled mountains (right) beckoning to be explored.

▶ TRAVELWISE

• **HOW TO VISIT** Twenty-five-minute flights from Honolulu and 1.75-hour ferry rides (*molokaiferry.com*) from Maui link Molokai to the outside world. The cliffs can be viewed on helicopter rides that originate at Maui (*bluehawaiian.com*), or for a closer-up view, the Kalaupapa Guided Mule Tour takes visitors down the cliffs to Kalaupapa National Historical Park via dozens of steep switchbacks (*muleride.com*).

• **PLANNING** Destination Molokai Visitors Association provides information on the island (*gohawaii.com/Molokai*); so does Kalaupapa National Historical Park (*nps.gov/kala*).

• **HOW TO STAY** Polynesian-inspired bungalows overlook the reef at Hotel Molokai on the south coast of the island (*hotelmolokai.com*).

Point Reyes National Seashore

It's not the sights, but the absence of sound that will first stop you in your tracks at Point Reyes National Seashore. Less than an hour before, you departed the clamorous, congested cities of the Bay Area. Now there's silence and space all around. The quietude focuses you on the beauty around you, an unspoiled vista where ocean meets land without the blight of an amusement pier anywhere.

Even on the most beautiful Northern California days, portions of the 71,000-acre (28,733 ha) park, with its 80 miles (129 km) of shoreline, remain uncrowded. Although it is accessible by road, the 11-mile (18 km) Great Beach—also known as Point Reyes Beach—can feel almost lonely, especially at its northern end where your only companion may be the endangered snowy plover. Here, the waves crash against the shore, and beware them—rip currents make this area dangerous for swimming. From many vantage points, the red-roofed Point Reyes Lighthouse at the southern tip of the beach, built in 1870, is the only evidence that anyone else has trod this stretch of oceanfront.

Drakes Beach, with its dramatic, striped white sandstone cliffs, is one of Point Reyes' most visited sites. Near one of the park's three visitors centers, the sheltered beach and its wide expanse of sand, washed by gentle surf, make it a favorite for day-trippers. If you go to the Chimney Rock overlook at the western edge of Drakes Bay during the winter months, you may catch sight of a breeding colony of elephant seals, or gray whales passing by in their annual migration.

From the visitors center, steps lead down to the Point Reyes Lighthouse (opposite), at the edge of the Pacific. The national seashore here includes Tomales Bay (above), edged by lush pastures.

A wave-washed beach on
Point Reyes, a peninsula
that's shaped like the head
of a seahorse

REWIND

National Geographic writer Frank Cameron drove California's coastal Highway One for a magazine article in the late 1950s, and parts of his account recall a long-departed time. Near the Golden Gate Bridge, he watched a ship towing a 50-foot (15 m) whale to one of the country's last whaling facilities, where it would be processed into oil and pet food. And 100 miles (160 km) north of Point Reyes, the 115-foot (35 m) Point Arena Lighthouse (pictured) sounded its foghorn constantly and signaled to ships offshore.

Picturesque as the 1907 lighthouse seemed, the Coast Guardsman on duty told Cameron ruefully, "You sit here for six hours straight with the foghorn blasting . . . Everything shakes and rattles. The wind howls. The only way to stretch your legs is to walk 135 steps up to the top. Me? I'll take a ship next tour of duty." The foghorn was silenced in the 1970s and an automatic light installed, and the keeper's quarters are vacation rentals today.

Farther off the beaten path is Wildcat Beach, accessible by an energetic 5.5-mile (9 km) hike along the Coastal Trail from the nearest road. From there, a mile's (1.6 km) walk south along the beach brings you to Alamere Falls. This rare tidefall roars down the coastal bluffs from a height of five stories, directly onto the beach. The sight of the broad cascade is most impressive in the rainier winter months. If you head north along Wildcat Beach, you might catch a glimpse of two "secret" falls, which flow only occasionally: Phantom Falls, a thin stream plummeting some 100 feet (30 m) down a sheer rock face, and Horsetail Falls, a three-story gusher. (This hike should only be attempted at low tide with a careful watch on the time: Hikers have been trapped here before.)

The seashore with its rhythmic waves can be hypnotic, but Point Reyes has far more to offer. Much of the park is filled with picturesque forests of towering Douglas firs and twisting bishop pines. Nearly 490 bird species stop off on the peninsula, and the park often attracts vagrants, migrating birds that are lost and unusual for the area. In early spring, the region blooms with colorful wildflowers—3-mile (5 km) Tomales Point Trail is one of the best hikes for viewing nature's bouquet. It winds through the Tule Elk

Reserve, and several more miles along a more challenging unmaintained trail brings you to a beautiful ocean overlook at the northernmost point of the park.

The park is also home to some more unexpected points of interest. Follow Sir Frances Drake Boulevard toward the Drakes Estero, and you'll see a small sign for North District Operations Center. Turn right to find a "tree tunnel" of gracefully arched cypresses—the sight is straight from an enchanted woodland. Continue along the path through the tunnel and you'll find one of the park's most interesting historic sites, an impressive RCA/Marconi wireless station. Built in 1929, the station was once a key part of ship-to-shore communications along the Pacific Rim, and

Monterey cypress trees draw you toward the RCA/Marconi Wireless Station KPH, built in 1929 and preserved at Point Reyes Beach.

in the 1940s, even quiet Point Reyes was abuzz with Morse code calls from World War II ships offshore (the station is open for tours many Saturdays, or by request).

As a finale, you should hike the short Earthquake Trail near the Bear Valley visitors center—you'll promptly find yourself atop the active San Andreas Fault. Along the trail sits a fence that runs perpendicular to the fault. Once continuous, the fence is now divided into two pieces that sit about 18 feet apart, evidence of the earth's shift along the fault during the famous 1906 earthquake.

▶ **TRAVELWISE**

• **HOW TO VISIT** Point Reyes National Seashore is best navigated by car—and further explored in hiking boots. Avoid the weekends between late December and early April, when a portion of the scenic Sir Francis Drake Boulevard is shuttle-bus only.

• **PLANNING** The National Park Service website has details on the national seashore, its sites, its wildlife, and advice on visiting (nps.gov/pore).

• **HOW TO STAY** Within the park, the only options are Hostelling International-Point Reyes or backcountry camping (permit required). Outside the park, there are many campgrounds and quaint B&Bs.

PICTURE
PERFECT

Foaming breakers wash over the rocky Point Reyes coastline near an isolated beach campsite, a mere 30 miles (48 km) north of San Francisco. Photographer Raul Touzon waited for the sun to sink in the late afternoon of a rare blue-sky day so the light was at a lower angle. "If you notice, the light and shadows on the ground lead [your eye] to the campsite," he says.

IMAGE BY RAUL TOUZON
National Geographic photographer

Canyonlands National Park

Over eons, the Green and Colorado Rivers cut sheer, sinuous gorges and canyons into the red-orange, arid landscape of southeastern Utah. Between these deep furrows rise huge mesas, narrow pillars, rock arches, and the lonely upright remnants of long-fallen canyon walls. This rugged terrain is Canyonlands National Park, and at its heart, the two rivers come to a confluence and flow south as the mighty Colorado.

Canyonlands is vast—it encompasses a whopping 337,598 acres (136,621 ha) and is divided into three districts: Island in the Sky, where a mesa rises high above the rivers' confluence; the Needles, hundreds of red- and tan-banded sandstone spires; and the Maze, a tortuous labyrinth of steep, high-walled canyons.

The Island in the Sky district is most accessible. Just past the main visitors center, the Shafer Canyon Overlook will give you an accurate first impression of this awesome, fiery landscape. From Island in the Sky mesa, it's 1,000 feet (305 m) down to the canyon floor and, if you look across to the eastern horizon, the snow-peaked La Sal Mountains will draw your gaze skyward. Look to your right, and you'll see the dirt White Rim Road plunging down into the canyon via a series of switchbacks with hair-raising exposures—this is one of those adventures that requires 4WD.

Farther along the main road, a turnoff for Upheaval Dome brings you to a short hike with an overlook of a 3-mile-wide (5 km)

Morning light brings out shades of pinks, both in the rock walls of Canyonlands National Park (opposite) and in the petals of the sego lily, Utah's state flower (above).

crater formation that is either an eroded salt dome or was created by a meteor 60 million years ago. The last stop on the main road is Grand View Point Overlook—take the 1-mile (1.6 km) hike along a narrow ridge of land to the tip of the Island in the Sky mesa for fabulous views in every direction.

The Needles District is more rugged, and is reached by a different entrance farther to the south. It is famous for the beautiful, striated pillars ("needles") of the Cedar Mesa Sandstone—a combination of uplift and erosion created these colorful, clustered columns. The Maze is the most difficult district to reach. Few roads penetrate this backcountry, and excursions into it usually entail multiple days. But if you make the effort, from the Maze Overlook, the vast, intricate rock puzzle of this region will be laid out before you from a perspective you'll get nowhere else. Northwest of the Maze, Horseshoe Canyon is a remote, day use area that has Native American rock art dating back thousands of years.

A visitor stands atop Mesa Arch in the aptly named Island in the Sky District of Canyonlands National Park (above). The Colorado River flows through the park (opposite).

▶ TRAVELWISE

- **HOW TO VISIT** The main access roads into Island in the Sky and Needles are paved. To get into the backcountry, you'll need to hike, mountain bike, or bring a high-clearance, 4WD vehicle. The most accessible district, Island in the Sky, is 40 minutes from Moab. Searing summer heat means spring and fall are the best months to explore.

- **PLANNING** The National Park Service website has maps of all the park districts, advice for exploring, and more on the park's campgrounds (nps.gov/cany).

- **HOW TO STAY** Canyonlands has no cabins or lodges. There are two campgrounds: Squaw Flat at the Needles and Willow Flat at Island in the Sky. The nearest hotels are in Moab, Monticello, or Hanksville, Utah.

Medicine Bow Peak

Few views of America's remote western mountains compare with the first glimpse of Wyoming's Snowy Mountain Range, around a bend on the lightly traveled 29-mile (47 km) Snowy Range Scenic Byway. Medicine Bow Peak, Sugarloaf Mountain, and Browns Peak all flash into view, with Medicine Bow's snow-blanketed summit—at 12,013 feet (3,662 m)—soaring above them all.

From the highest point on the byway, the 10,847-foot (3,306 m) Snowy Range Pass, visitors should walk to the Libby Flats Observation Site. On crystal-clear days, it's possible to stand at the overlook, stare south, and see as far away as Colorado's Rawah and Never Summer Wilderness Areas. But a bit farther west on the byway is the bend in the road that serves as the most picturesque entry to the range: In the calm waters of three glacial lakes is the reflection of the magnificent Medicine Bow Peak, which itself rears steeply skyward, covered with powder-white ridges and snowfields that persist on the slopes almost year-round.

According to lore, Native American tribes gathered in this area to hold healing ceremonies and build weapons. Settlers combined "making medicine" and "making bows" to coin the name Medicine Bow. Even at the height of summer, the Snowy Mountain Range, true to its name, can make for chilly camping amid residual snowdrifts and brisk daytime temps. In warmer weather, the snow retreats from the mountain's south face and bursts of color—including pink-hued "watermelon" snow (the color is produced

Spectacular views of the Rocky Mountains of Colorado unfold to the south of Medicine Bow Peak (opposite).
The Snowy Range has wildlife like elk, black bear, and red fox (above).

by algae in the glacial snow)—paint the lower elevations of Medicine Bow.

Hike to the peak for solitude and panoramic views of the surrounding Snowy Range to the north, Longs Peak and Mount Zirkel to the south, and the jewel-like alpine lakes below. Trail options range from easy to expert, but all require navigating some rocky, scree-littered, and steep sections. One of the most gradual summit routes begins at the 10,480-foot (3,194 m) elevation Lake Marie trailhead and travels 3.6 miles (6 km) to the top. Check weather conditions before hiking because summer storms can come on fast and are a serious danger to hikers caught out on the treeless slopes.

July and August are best for seeing Medicine Bow Peak's alpine valleys blanketed with columbine and Indian paintbrush. This is also the only time of year to comfortably camp (even then, prepare for freezing nighttime temps). Sugarloaf Campground fills up quickly on summer weekends, but the campsites on the northwest side of the loop offer stunning views of Medicine Bow Peak.

A winter day's last rays glow on the rock faces of the Snowy Range and in Mirror Lake (opposite). The mountains are accessed by the lightly traveled Snowy Range Scenic Byway (above).

▶ TRAVELWISE

- **HOW TO VISIT** Drive the Snowy Range Scenic Byway (WY 130) east to west between Laramie and Saratoga in southeastern Wyoming. The byway is typically open Memorial Day to mid-October (weather permitting), but if you try to hike before July, you'll be traversing a lot of snow. To hike the peak, park at the Mirror Lake Picnic Site.

- **PLANNING** Stop at the Centennial Visitors Center (about 30 miles/48 km west of Laramie) for byway and trail maps (*wyomingtourism.org; visitlaramie.org*).

- **HOW TO STAY** Originally a stagecoach stop, the historic Hotel Wolf in downtown Saratoga, about 35 miles (56 km) west, has welcomed travelers, cowboys, and probably a few outlaws since 1893. There are 10 rooms and an Old West saloon (*wolfhotel.com*).

MONTANA

National Bison Range

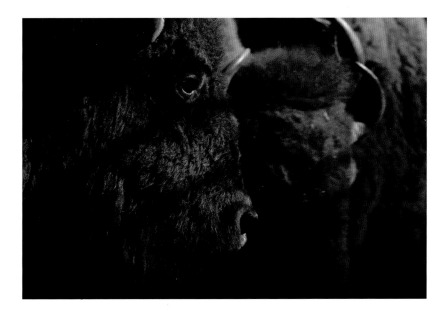

Five hundred years ago, more than 30 million bison grazed the North American prairies, from the Appalachians to the Rockies, and the Gulf Coast to Alaska. In those days, the land that is now the American West was sparsely populated by people, and was a rolling grassland where bison herds roamed beneath snowcapped peaks. The view from the top of Red Sleep Mountain in Montana's National Bison Range is nearly unchanged.

When the American pioneers began settling the West, the continent's bison herds were hunted nearly into extinction. By the end of the 19th century, there were estimated to be barely 1,000 of the animals left. In 1908, afraid they would die out entirely, Theodore Roosevelt established the National Bison Range, 18,500 acres (7,487 ha) in northwestern Montana where the animals would be protected and could live in a natural environment.

What began as a small herd of 40 bison is now a thriving population of 350 to 500 animals.

The dozen miles (19 km) of often narrow gravel roadways that wind through the range are nearly the only evidence of modern-day incursion on this land. From these roads and a few short trails, visitors—only about 130,000 a year—can observe the bison and other animals through the seasons.

The hulking American bison (above) once roamed the Mountain West in massive herds before being brought to near extinction. Today it is once again a presence in the parks and ranges of the western United States—including the hills of Montana's National Bison Range (opposite).

Fastest of all land mammals in **North America**, the pronghorn antelope can reach speeds of **60** miles an hour (**96 kph**).

Although the range is open year-round, its most spectacular pass, Red Sleep Mountain Drive, is closed in winter. Traditionally (and weather permitting), the road reopens on Mother's Day weekend each spring, a particularly lively time on the range. The grasslands bloom with brilliant native wildflowers like yellow bells and paintbrush. The bluebirds and meadowlarks arrive as early as March and sing through the spring. And the star attraction: Bison calves are born mid-April to mid-May—you can admire their rusty red coats and knock-kneed gambols, but beware their very protective one-ton mothers.

In the hot summer months, bighorn sheep can often be spotted at the higher altitudes along Red Sleep Mountain Drive, especially near High Point, a 1-mile (1.6 km) walking loop. The half-mile (0.8 km) Bitterroot Trail is the place to see the state's official flower, the purple-pink bitterroot (*Lewisia rediviva*) that peeks between the rocks on sunny days. As its botanical name suggests, Lewis and Clark are credited with first collecting the flower, though the American Indians had been using it in their diet for generations. Black bears forage for berries along Pauline Creek, though you're more likely to hear the solitary, shy animals than to see them. Prairie Drive takes you along Mission Creek, prime for spotting white-tailed deer in the mornings and evenings.

By fall, the trees and grasses of this country turn golden and snow starts falling. September to October is elk mating season, and the area along Mission Creek is the best place to see and hear the noisy, distinctive courting rituals of the male elk.

But even as snow covers the grassland and many birds head south for the winter, the rough-legged hawks and bald eagles swoop over the range. During January and February, great horned owls begin their mating rituals, and along the 1-mile (1.6 km) nature trail, you may glimpse these powerful birds. They have a wingspan that can top 4 feet (1.2 m), and they glower at the world from under matching feathery tufts that resemble "horns." Their lonesome calls drift across the grasslands at dusk in early winter, and in the distance, coyotes yip, breaking the icy still of this remote land. The only human sound you'll hear is your own breathing.

▶ TRAVELWISE

• **HOW TO VISIT** The National Bison Range entrance is located off Highway 212. The well-maintained gravel roads can be navigated by car; larger vehicles and trailers are prohibited on most roads. The range is open year-round from dawn to dusk, though Red Sleep Mountain Drive is closed early October until mid-May.

• **PLANNING** Information about the landscape, wildlife, and conditions at the range are on the Forest Service website (*fws.gov/refuge/ National_Bison_Range*).

• **HOW TO STAY** There are some small hotels, motels, and campgrounds on Route 93, but the nearest town of any real size is Polson, an hour north by car. The city of Missoula is slightly farther to the south.

REWIND ALBINO BISON ON THE RANGE

This image of a rare albino bison is archived in the National Geographic collections, though it was published in *Natural History* magazine in April 1940. W. Peyton Moncure, a photographer for Yellowstone National Park, submitted the photo. He had spotted this magnificent and very rare creature on the National Bison Range in Montana and was greatly affected by its appearance and confidence. "He is a bold animal," Moncure wrote, "and at the sight of us, he came unhesitatingly forward down the side of the hillock, the others following him more uncertainly." Moncure remarked on the seven-year-old animal's pure white coat and red eyes, "There is something else strange, and one might say, diabolic in his appearance."

This bison sired an albino calf that was born blind. The handicapped offspring lived in less free-roaming splendor—but in much greater safety and comfort—in the confines of the Smithsonian National Zoo in Washington, D.C.

The hills of the National Bison Range are covered with wildflowers in spring, and roamed by black bears, coyotes—and of course, bison.

PICTURE
PERFECT

A bison thunders over the prairie in Montana's National Bison Range. Photographer Lowell Georgia took this shot during the herd's mating season in late summer, when the bulls are particularly aggressive. "This bull had just wallowed in dust and was preparing for his charge, not at me, but a bull off to my right," says Georgia, who was on assignment for a National Geographic book on animal behavior. "Both bulls charge and just before impact raise up and ram skulls at full force. That clash of skulls is a very loud cracking sound."

IMAGE BY LOWELL GEORGIA
National Geographic photographer

Sable Island

Over the centuries, this windswept island off the coast of Canada has been called by many names, most recently Sable Island National Park Reserve. But it is the island's sober nickname—the Graveyard of the Atlantic—that provokes respect in mariners of every nationality, and gives modern visitors a sense of just how remote and wild this sliver of sand in the North Atlantic really is.

As you approach from the Canadian mainland, Sable Island appears through a shroud of fog in the distance, a crescent of emerald and alabaster, surrounded by a vast sea. Wild horses gambol along the margins of inland ponds or climb steep dune paths. Herds of plump seals bask in the sun or plunge frenetically into the sea. Lines of turquoise breakers froth against the beaches. Standing on one of the only emerging parts of the North American continental shelf, 180 miles (290 km) east-southeast of Nova Scotia,

Sable Island stretches 26 miles (42 km) from tip to tip and is a mere 0.8 mile (1.3 km) wide. In the 1880s, naturalists predicted that within 100 years, Sable Island would be swallowed by the stormy waters of the North Atlantic. So far, time has proved them wrong.

This is an island barely inhabited by people, unless you count a handful of hardy researchers, scientists, and Parks Canada employees. A wind sock flying from the bumper of a truck and orange construction cones mark the runway of the island's "airport."

Sable Island (opposite), barely a strand of earth in the vast North Atlantic, is home to some 500 wild horses (above).
The stocky feral horses are descendants of those released on the island in the late 18th century.

Visitation is restricted by both Parks Canada and Mother Nature, and in 2015, Sable Island saw only 120 visitors.

Remote, difficult to access, and dangerous, Sable Island was first mapped in the 1500s by the Portuguese and was surveyed by the British in the late 1700s. But maps alone could not prevent the more than 350 recorded shipwrecks off the island's coast, doomed vessels that fell prey to rough seas, dense fogs, treacherous currents, and hidden sandbars that extend out from the island. Several colonizing expeditions hoping to reap the wealth of the island's furs and fish also failed. Not until 1801 was Sable Island permanently settled with a most necessary lifesaving station.

A natural haven for its indigenous populations of seals and birds, Sable Island is home to the largest breeding colony of gray seals in the world (about 50,000), and is the only nesting grounds of the Ipswich sparrow. In 1977, the entire island was designated a migratory bird sanctuary. Although they no longer blacken the sky as they did a hundred years ago, the flyway welcomes over 2,500 pairs of terns each summer. (Walking near nesting terns is highly discouraged; they can be vicious.)

Over the past 400 years, an eclectic group of imports including horses, cattle, pigs, sheep, foxes, rabbits, and rodents left their mark on Sable's fragile ecosystem. Of these, only Sable Island's most

Sable Island is home to the world's largest breeding colony of gray seals. Most pups arrive from late December to early February.

Alexander Graham Bell, then president of the National Geographic Society, came to Sable Island with his wife Mabel on a sad mission in 1898. True to its name, the "Graveyard of the Atlantic" had buried the French ocean liner *La Bourgogne* 60 miles (97 km) off the coast of Sable. It collided with another ship in dense fog and sank, taking with it 550 passengers and crew. Mr. and Mrs. Bell had come to the island to search in vain for two shipwrecked friends. The Bells were unaware the photographer had crept up behind them to take this poignant photo.

Bell's grandson was transfixed by his grandfather's stories of the island—"He saw wrecks of ships littering the beaches and 'wild ponies dashing down upon the shore into the midst of hundreds of seals.'" Nearly 70 years later, the younger Bell went back to Sable on his own *National Geographic* assignment—and on that trip, photographer William Allard captured the shot on pp. 56–57.

lighthouse keeper's collapsed home; a decommissioned lighthouse. Modern navigational systems have made shipwrecks less of a peril, and today a modern observation tower monitors the long-range transport of pollution aerosols through the upper atmosphere. This tiny scimitar of sand now embraces its newest challenge, mapping one of the world's modern threats—a changing climate.

TRAVELWISE

• **HOW TO VISIT** August to October is the optimal window. Sable Island is an extremely isolated location, and access to it depends on the weather. Visitors arrive either by air charter (*maritimeair.com*) or come ashore from private vessels that are anchored offshore.

• **PLANNING** Parks Canada requires all visitors to register in advance of their trip. Its website has good information for those planning a visit (*pc.gc.ca/eng/pn-np/ns/sable/index.aspx*).

• **HOW TO STAY** To date, visits are limited to day trips. Visitors fly to and from the island on the same day or spend the night in a vessel anchored offshore.

famous residents—the feral horses—remain, and number around 500. These free-running herds have adapted to a diet of marram grass and are sustained by freshwater ponds. They have lived undisturbed by humans since the 1960s, when the island's lighthouses became automated, and are unused to seeing people even now.

The ghosts of the island are visible to keen-eyed visitors: an anchor or gravestone exposed by waves or the ever shifting sands; the ribs of a ship jutting out from a sand dune; the bones of a

PICTURE
PERFECT

In 1947, the freighter *Manhasset* wrecked on a sandbar off the coast of Sable Island. Years later, William Allard took this shot of the ship's mast rising above the sea, marking its watery gravesite. This photo is from very early in Allard's career, on his first assignment outside the United States. He was struck by Sable's remoteness. "There was a man and wife living on the island, along with maybe a half dozen government employees running a weather station," he recalls. "One could not get off the island until a ship of some size was due to bring in supplies."

**IMAGE BY
WILLIAM ALBERT ALLARD**
National Geographic photographer

Ilulissat Icefjord

Off the western coast of Greenland, land of the midnight sun, the Ilulissat Icefjord seems a two-chromed world of white and blue, nothing but the cool shades of ice, water, and sky. Then the sun begins to set—a leisurely process that's never quite complete in summer—and the chilly scenery is transformed. The towering icebergs begin to glow red and orange, an effect heightened by the reflections of the calm, silvery water.

The Ilulissat Icefjord is a rare, ice-choked tidal fjord at the mouth of the Sermeq Kujalleq glacier in Greenland, 155 miles (250 km) north of the Arctic Circle. The fast-moving glacier calves constantly, sending massive chunks of ice roaring into the waters of the fjord with a series of cracks and booms. Sermeq Kujalleq (also known as Jakobshavn Isbræ) by most estimates sheds 10 percent of all the calf ice produced in Greenland every year. It is believed that the iceberg that sank the *Titanic* started here. More recently,

in August 2015, this glacier calved a massive iceberg 5 miles square (13 sq km) into the fjord, a behemoth bound gradually for the frigid waters of the North Atlantic.

One of the best ways to try to fathom the vastness of the glacier and Ilulissat Icefjord—the fjord itself is around 4 miles (6 km) wide and 34 miles (55 km) long—is from overhead, by helicopter or fixed-wing plane. By sea, a ship that seemed substantial in port feels diminutive next to the icebergs, some of which are as tall as

One of the most productive glaciers in the world, the Sermeq Kujalleq (opposite) produces 10 percent of the calf ice shed in Greenland each year. The colorful town of Ilulissat (above) is near the glacier and icefjord.

skyscrapers. The mass and power of these huge slabs of ice, breaking away from the glacier, roiling the sea, then drifting and colliding on their way out to the open water, is awesome. But it is perhaps by land, hiking at your own leisure through the countryside, that you find yourself most affected by the scene. The famed Blue Route trail, a 4.25-mile (7 km) trek, skirts the bank of Ilulissat Icefjord. As you scramble over rocks, free of the buzz of plane engines or the crash ocean waves make against a ship's hull, the shifting, shearing, and movement of the ice is most audible. Some people say you can even smell it—a sharp, fresh, elusive scent that's probably different for everyone. It is here too that you can see the evening sun change the frosty landscape into a warm, pink- and yellow-hued spectacle, the ragged bergs deep blue silhouettes against a golden sky.

Nature would seem to be in charge here. The cheerful town of Ilulissat (the name means "icebergs") is Greenland's third largest, but it has only about 4,500 residents. Even if you add its population of around 3,500 sled dogs, it is a mere speck on this northern expanse of white.

Greenland huskies (above) have two layers of fur: an inner wool-like layer and a longer outer water-repellent coat. These make them well able to withstand the icy landscape above the Arctic Circle (opposite).

▶ TRAVELWISE

• **HOW TO VISIT** The town of Ilulissat is the starting point for any adventure in the icefjord. The town is accessible by plane or, in good weather, by boat. Summer provides the best opportunity and ample daylight for exploring the icefjord. Between September and March, the northern lights are often visible. In the winter, a dogsled ride is a must.

• **PLANNING** The government-backed Visit Greenland's website is the best one-stop site for planning a trip to the country and Ilulissat (green land.com).

• **HOW TO STAY** Ilulissat has the largest concentration of hotels in Greenland, but reservations are recommended.

MEXICO

Chiapas

Mexico's Chiapas state is a trove of geological wonders, exotic wildlife, and ancient ruins. On the eastern side of the state are the remains of the ancient Mayan city of Palenque, with stunning temples and pyramids. Farther west is one of the region's crown jewels, Sima de las Cotorras, a gargantuan limestone sinkhole named for its vivid, raucous inhabitants: *cotorras*, or green parakeets.

Emerging from the mists of the jungle in the northeastern part of Chiapas is the ancient Mayan city of Palenque, home to around 6,000 people at its height in A.D. 600. Forests of mahogany and cedar surround these impressive ruins, which are considered some of the best examples of Mayan culture, architecture, and sculpture still standing. The most striking building, the Temple of the Inscriptions, sits atop a massive stepped pyramid and has walls covered with hieroglyphic inscriptions. In 1952, archaeologists discovered beneath it the tomb of the ruler-priest Pakal, who

was laid to rest among a wealth of jade ornaments and trinkets.

About 43 miles (70 km) south, a natural spectacle no less entrancing interrupts the dense jungle vegetation—Agua Azul, a series of cascading waterfalls, tumbling terrace over terrace and almost unbelievably azure, thanks to streambeds of limestone and travertine.

Farther west in Chiapas is a beautiful, bizarre quirk of the region's geology. This area is grooved by fissures and depressions created by subterranean water seeping through the limestone of the Sierra Madre mountain range over millennia. The most stunning of these

formations is a dizzying, circular cavity nearly the length of a football field and 45 stories deep: the Sima de las Cotorras.

The sinkhole might seem a frightful pit if not for the oasis of mature sapodilla, copal, and Maya breadnut trees that blanket its bottom. Each morning at dawn, the sinkhole releases a plume of emerald-feathered birds that emerge like a cyclone up toward the sky. After a day of feasting on grubs and seeds aboveground, the squawking parrots swoop back into the sinkhole and take roost for the night in the trees and the nooks of the limestone walls. These twice-a-day performances are typically at their height from March to October—the rest of the year the parrots tend to decamp to warmer, lowland climes.

The relationship between parrot and sinkhole is mutually beneficial: The sinkhole shelters the parrots from most predators, and the birds deposit seeds they've collected during the day onto the floor of the yawning pit. Like a giant terrarium, the sinkhole traps humidity and creates a balmy microclimate for the trees to grow. It is not uncommon for trees in the sinkhole to reach nearly 100 feet (30 m) in height, nearly twice the height they may reach aboveground.

Evidence of pre-Hispanic exploration of the sinkhole has been inscribed on its walls. Dozens of ancient rock paintings have been found on a ledge halfway up the sinkhole, including handprints and human and animal figures. Most historians agree they belong

Trees growing from the base of the Sima de las Cotorras reach nearly 100 feet (30 m) in height, thanks to the sinkhole's terrarium effect.

REWIND A HEAD IN THE JUNGLE

In the 1940s, archaeologist Matthew Stirling led eight National Geographic- and Smithsonian-sponsored expeditions to southern Mexico. His team discovered awesome remnants from La Venta, a major cultural and political center of the Olmec, the first great civilization of Mesoamerica.

The expedition penetrated ravines and shimmied down sinkholes, uncovering long-lost human and animal effigies, altars, terraced mounds, and ball courts. Intrigued by rumors of vine-enshrouded statues, the expedition ventured into the jungle outside La Venta, in the state of Tabasco. There, they uncovered 11 enormous stone heads, including this one, called El Rey (pictured are Stirling's wife and excavation workers). Carved from lava rock and estimated at over 30 tons, El Rey was the largest and best preserved—"the colossal head to end all colossal heads," Stirling noted reverently. The team conjectured that iconoclasts had sought to destroy the monuments of La Venta. Luckily, El Rey was so massive that the worst they could do was roll him into a ditch.

To the west of the two sinkholes, the Río la Venta loosely forms the southwestern border of the Reserva Biosfera de la Selva del Ocote, home to such rare species as the critically endangered howler monkey and tapir, jaguars, pumas, ocelot, and even the rare-to-Mexico river crocodile.

TRAVELWISE

• **HOW TO VISIT** The major airport in Chiapas is in Tuxtla Gutiérrez. To reach Sima de las Cotorras, you can join a tour group that picks visitors up in downtown Tuxtla. San Cristóbal de las Casas, about 40 miles (64 km) east, is a good central base for visiting the rest of Chiapas state.

• **PLANNING** The Mexico Tourism Board website has info for sites like Palenque (visitmexico.com). To explore further afield, tour group Ecobiosfera El Triunfo offers bird tours of El Ocote (ecobiosfera.org.mx).

• **HOW TO STAY** A rustic hotel sits on the edge of the sinkhole and serves meals with a view. Rooms and rappelling excursions can be reserved through Sima de las Cotorras Ecoturismo (simaecoturismo.com).

to the indigenous Zoque people, and estimates for some of the more recent paintings range from 1,000 to 10,000 years old. Though the meaning of the paintings remains a mystery, what is certain is that the artists risked life and limb to create them.

Experienced climbers may find the sheer walls of the sinkhole navigable, but the vast majority of visitors opt to rappel them with the help of one of several local tour companies. Just a 30-minute hike from Sima de las Cotorras lies another smaller sinkhole, Sima del Mujú, with its own gallery of ancient rock paintings.

PICTURE
PERFECT

In a cacophony of squawks, a cloud of emerald green parrots flits about the opening of Mexico's Sotano de las Golondrinas, or "Pit of Swallows." Most bird lovers perch on the edge of this deep vertical cave to see the eponymous swallows, which leave the sinkhole at dawn to forage for food. "The surprise to me was that there was also a large population of green parrots that live in the cave," says photographer Stephen Alvarez. "I used a long shutter speed to both compensate for the low light and to provide a sense of movement to the birds' flight."

IMAGE BY STEPHEN ALVAREZ
National Geographic photographer

COSTA RICA

Orosí Valley

The Orosí Valley is what you picture when you think of Costa Rica. Volcanoes loom in the distance, steep hillsides are planted with coffee, a single road encircles a secluded, lush green valley dotted with red roofs, and in one of those small towns, a simple, whitewashed church has a history that dates back centuries to Spanish colonial times.

The Orosí Valley in central Costa Rica is reached by a beautiful drive, an hour-and-a-half ramble by car from the capital of San José, past coffee plantations, volcanoes, and verdant landscape. The Reventazon River weaves through the Orosí Valley, and life along the broad, brisk tributary has a restful quality—directions are given by landmarks and time is marked by the bus schedule. To the west of the valley are the foothills of the Cordillera de Talamanca; to the east sit the active volcanoes of the Cordillera Central. Perhaps the most striking of these is Irazú Volcano, the highest in Costa Rica—it last erupted in 1963 and a blue-green lake fills one of its two craters.

The valley's two towns flank the Reventazon. On the eastern edge of the valley, the town of Ujarras sits at the edge of Lake Cachi, which was created by damming the Reventazon in the 1970s. The original town was destroyed in a flood in 1833; today, the evocative ruins of one of Costa Rica's oldest churches (believed to have been built in the 1600s) remain, and are surrounded by a garden that invites rest and contemplation.

The rocky Rio Grande de Orosí (opposite) is one of hundreds of rivers rushing through Costa Rica's tranquil Orosí Valley. Rich local coffee (above) is grown on high-altitude plantations.

At the valley's southern tip is the village of Orosí, home to the Iglesia de San José de Orosí, built in the 1700s and still the country's oldest active church. The low, colonial architecture is humble and striking in its simplicity—adobe walls, terra-cotta floor, and a gilt wood altar—and the church houses a small museum. Both towns are good starting points for exploring the valley's wilds.

Parque Nacional Tapantí is the Orosí Valley at its most pristine. Seven miles (11 km) from Orosí town center, through coffee plantations, the park is the rainiest patch of Costa Rica and sees more than 20 feet (6 m) of precipitation each year. Though trails extend only a short distance into the 19-square-mile (50 sq km) refuge, there is plenty to see. The Árboles Caídos Trail is the best bet for spotting some of the park's animals, which include such exotic creatures as monkeys, jaguars, and anteaters. Listen for the rhythmic song of the resplendent quetzal. The aqua- or lime-colored bird is sacred in Mayan culture, and has long been a symbol of freedom. It can occasionally be spotted near the ranger station.

The Orosí Valley has attractions both man-made and natural, from the Iglesia de San José de Orosí (above), to the tropical forest of Macizo de la Muerte, where tree limbs are covered with epiphytes (right).

▶ TRAVELWISE

- **HOW TO VISIT** The valley is accessible by car or by bus from Cartago, about 40 minutes away. A car is useful for exploring the valley, though there are also opportunities for hiking and horseback riding. Parque Nacional Tapantí is best visited February through April, the least rainy season.

- **PLANNING** The Orosí Valley tourism site (in Spanish only) has info on dining, staying, and exploring in the valley (orosivalley.com).

- **HOW TO STAY** The valley has numerous small lodges and bed-and-breakfasts. A 15-person cabin is available in Parque Nacional Tapantí.

Water is the defining
characteristic of the
Pantanal, a vast inland
delta spreading from Brazil
to Paraguay and Bolivia.

South America

This is a continent of rare sights—flat-topped mountains rising above the clouds, elusive jaguars, 20-story palm trees, and vibrantly colored desert hills.

VENEZUELA

Mount Roraima

Near the boundary of the Amazon and Orinoco Basins, where Brazil, Guyana, and Venezuela meet, an ancient, anvil-shaped mountain looms out of the jungle. Mount Roraima, with its phantasmagoric landscape and untamable greenery, prompted early European explorers to declare it inaccessible. But climb it you can, and the reward from the top is thick clouds parting like a biblical sea to reveal a panorama of other mesas and savanna pastures expanding across three countries.

The massive sandstone mesa Mount Roraima is one of the tallest tepuis, or tabletop mountains, scattered across the Guiana Highlands in Venezuela and western Guyana. The word "tepui" is loosely translated as "sprouting rock" in the indigenous Pemón language, spoken by the indigenous people of this part of South America. And so it seems—the mountain's flat top rises almost vertically 9,217 feet (2,809 m) above sea level. A popular trail starts in Paraitepui and ascends to the top of Roraima—this is the route British botanist Sir Everard im Thurn used with his Guyanese guides in 1884, when he achieved the first European ascent. It is at times slippery and steep, but still a doable hike for a fit, patient amateur without climbing gear. Hikers taking on the weeklong journey (three days to traverse the surrounding savanna and climb to the summit, two nights on the top, and then two days down) will encounter a paradoxical ecosystem that can seem both punishing and luxuriant at the same time. Sticky, warm air hangs

Tabletop mountains, or tepuis, such as **Mount Roraima** (opposite) offer spectacular vantage points for hikers hardy enough to get to the top. Plants adapted to the region include leatherwood (*Cyrilla racemiflora*, above).

closely about the dense cloud forests, unrelenting *jejene* sand flies swarm the mountain's slopes, and rain falls abundantly. The heavy precipitation feeds the Orinoco, Negro, and Essequibo Rivers.

Water gushes from the mountain plateau in frothing white waterfalls, pouring over the near-vertical flanks before disappearing into the thick vegetation below. Mount Roraima's greenery is such a dense tangle that it has inspired some fantastical tales, including Sir Arthur Conan Doyle's *The Lost World* (1912), in which stegosaurs and pterodactyls survive into the modern day on an otherworldly plateau in South America. (In actuality, nobody has discovered any lingering prehistoric megafauna on Roraima . . . yet.)

In other places, the mountain's rocky, precipitous terrain seems so barren that one wonders how it could host life at all. But even in an extreme climate that swings from hot and muggy to cold and clammy, some species have adapted to thrive in this challenging highland environment. Pebble-size black Roraima bush toads camouflage themselves between shrubbery and rocks, evading the tarantulas that long to devour them. In rain-drenched crevices thrive plants like flute-shaped sun pitchers, tentacled sundews, butterflylike bladderworts, and bromeliads—all delicate looking, yet voraciously carnivorous.

But no other plant thrives in Mount Roraima's unforgiving environment like the orchid. These elegant flowers flourish in

Mount Roraima, soaring above the clouds, is a remnant of Pangaea, the supercontinent that included both South America and Africa.

Dr. Henry Edward Crampton, a curator at the American Museum of Natural History, undertook an arduous eight-week expedition from Georgetown, Guyana, to Mount Roraima and wrote about it for *National Geographic* in 1920. When his team got to Kaieteur Falls in Guyana (pictured), Crampton was awed: "The magnificence and impressiveness of the scene are immeasurably greater than words can convey. Over the red-brown cliffs at the head of the chasm pours a vast sheet of water more than 800 feet in height . . . The waters pour down into the depths with a tremendous roar, to be heard for miles around."

Perhaps nearly as awesome—to the Arecuna, an indigenous people of Venezuela—was the sight of Crampton later performing a traditional *paiwari* dance to ease tensions between his team and the local inhabitants. "The sight of the bearded, spectacled, and khaki-clad stranger solemnly performing in such a manner was too much for their sense of humor," Crampton related. The Arecuna dissolved into good-natured laughter.

top of Roraima, rock arches lead to menacing stone formations that resemble sculpted stone monsters, and the pursuit of glittering quartz deposits may lure you into a sinkhole. You wouldn't want to get lost up there—and to prevent it, no individual traveler is permitted on Roraima without an experienced tour guide.

TRAVELWISE

• **HOW TO VISIT** Mount Roraima, although accessible from Brazil and Guyana, is most easily scaled from Venezuela's Canaima National Park. Guides can be booked in Santa Elena, the nearest city in Venezuela, or Boa Vista in Brazil, which has flight connections to North America via Manaus and Rio de Janeiro. The rainy season can be a challenging time on unpaved trails. December through April is best time to visit.

• **PLANNING** Tour operators include Brazilian and Venezuelan outfitters (*roraima-brasil.com.br; newfrontiersadventures.com*).

• **HOW TO STAY** Many tours leave from Santa Elena in Venezuela, where you can stay at Posada L'Auberge (*l-auberge.net*) with creature comforts like hot water and Wi-Fi. You'll find even cushier options in Boa Vista, Brazil, including Aipana Plaza Hotel (*aipanaplaza.com.br/main*).

wind-carved fissures, turning Roraima into one of South America's greatest concentrations of orchids. On the mountain's sides, blanketed in cloud forest, and on its wind-battered summit, a wide range of these flowers absorb nutrients from the sandstone soil and use the windy heights to disperse dustlike seeds. The orchids range in size from blossoms that can reach 6 inches (15 cm), to flowers the size of pen tips. New species are constantly discovered.

Even inanimate objects like rocks can seem dynamic in this lofty, isolated landscape. In the Daliesque maze of stones on the

PICTURE
PERFECT

A female, thumb-size pebble toad clutches a tree branch in the dense, wet jungle of southwestern Guyana's Pakaraima Mountains. "They're nearly impossible to see," says photographer Joe Riis, who spent two months on assignment in Guyana, living in sodden tents and documenting the lifetime work of herpetologist Bruce Means, who was always on the lookout for rare or new species. "I would first listen for their calls then walk toward the sound." And if you think the females are small, the males are half their size.

IMAGE BY JOE RIIS
National Geographic photographer

Pantanal

The Amazon's alter ego is a massive wilderness area called the Pantanal that sprawls across southern Brazil and parts of two neighboring nations. The world's largest tropical wetland is home to a vast array of life. More than anything else, the great morass is renowned as the best place on Earth to catch a glimpse of the elusive jaguar, with its distinctive rosette-covered coat and sleek, powerful physique.

Ten times larger than Florida's celebrated Everglades, the Pantanal is basically a vast inland delta, a mosaic of rivers and marshes, savanna grasslands and tropical forest, and hundreds of lakes. During a rainy season that runs between November and April, around 80 percent of the wetlands are covered in water. The Paraguay River channels much of this to the South Atlantic, but a good amount lingers in the Pantanal Basin, providing year-round sustenance for an astounding number of plants and animals. Scientists figure hundreds more have yet to even be identified.

The jaguar occupies the top of the food chain and is one of the few felines that takes to water. The best way to see one is on a boat trip—these big cats are not averse to swimming, and are sometimes seen crossing rivers. The wetlands harbor many other strange creatures little known and rarely seen outside the Pantanal. These include the giant river otter, which can weigh as much as a German shepherd; the tamandua anteater with panda-like markings and giant hooked claws; and the yellow anaconda, a black dappled serpent that can grow as long as a pickup truck.

Orange-tipped fish (opposite) swirl just below the water's surface at Balneario Municipal de Bonito in Brazil; on land, *pantaneiros* ("cowboys," above) herd cattle.

Humans have coexisted with the wetlands for thousands of years and continue to be a key part of a visitor's Pantanal experience. Local fishermen take to the waters in dugout canoes while *Pantaneiros* ("cowboys") herd their hump-backed zebu cattle on ranches around the wilderness periphery.

Brazil's Pantanal Matogrossense National Park and three private reserves comprise UNESCO's Pantanal Conservation Area. Across the border, Rio Negro National Park in Paraguay and several small reserves in eastern Bolivia safeguard other parts of the wetlands. Cuiabá is the northern gateway to the Pantanal region. From there, the Transpantaneira Highway shoots south into the swamps. Driving the largely unpaved 90-mile (145 km) route is an adventure all its own, with cowboys herding their cattle down the track and wildlife shooting across the road. It terminates at Porto Jofre on the Cuiabá River, jumping-off point for many of the boat trips that explore the region.

The immense waterways of the Pantanal (opposite) provide an ideal habitat for jaguars (above), the largest of South America's big cats, and good swimmers.

▶ TRAVELWISE

• **HOW TO VISIT** Guided river trips are the best way to discover the Pantanal and its wild inhabitants. Wilderness lodges provide day trips while experienced outfitters like Terra Incognita Ecotours *(ecotours .com)* offer multiday land and water adventures.

• **PLANNING** Pantanal Escapes' online guide offers travel advice and background information about the Pantanal *(pantanalescapes.com)*.

• **HOW TO STAY** Visitors can choose from a mix of wilderness lodges, small hotels *(pousadas)* and ranches *(fazendas)*. Hotel Porto Jofre *(portojofre.com.br)* is located deeper in the swamps than any other accommodation. On the south side of the Pantanal, Hotel Fazenda Baía das Pedras *(baiadaspedras.com.br/ing)* is a working ranch that also organizes wildlife tours.

Valle de Cocora

Sheltered within the Andean cloud forest and coffee plantations of central Colombia, the emerald green valley of Valle de Cocora appears more like an ethereal vision than an earthly preserve. Heightening this quality are hundreds of lofty, nearly evenly spaced wax palms, national symbol of Colombia and the world's tallest palm. The highest of the slim, pole-like trees towers at the height of a 20-story building.

When the palms' fringed frond tops are blanketed by fog or blocked by brilliant sun, the bare, pale gray trunks resemble spindly bird legs supporting a vast, unseen flock. A visit to Valle de Cocora—considered the best place in the world to see the wax palms in the wild—is a rare opportunity to walk among these strange giants. The lush grassland valley is carpeted with a low, vivid green and dips gently between rippling, forested hills. It is named Cocora ("star of water") for the Quimbayan princess, and is uniquely suited to support the trees. A combination of high altitude (ranging from 5,900 to 7,874 feet/1,798 to 2,400 m above sea level), nearly daily rainfall, and highly acidic soil creates a nourishing environment for the trees. Other native Andean highlands' flora that flourishes here includes the flowering *encenillo* tree and the *puya,* a spiky bromeliad with thick, waxy leaves.

In historically Roman Catholic Colombia, the wax palms' huge fronds were once used in annual Palm Sunday masses. Between the palm fronds being harvested each spring and locals cutting down the trees for building materials, the wax palms were nearly

The cloud-blanketed valley of Cocora (opposite) is a good place to spot toucans (above), hummingbirds, trogons, and other tropical birds.

wiped out by the early 1980s. To protect the trees from extinction—which in turn endangered the yellow-eared parrot that roosts, nests, and feeds in the palms—the government designated the Valle de Cocora a part of Los Nevados National Natural Park in 1985.

Valle de Cocora is one of the most accessible areas in the 225-square-mile (58,300 ha) park. Horseback riding on the valley's trails is particularly popular among vacationing Colombians. Near the trailhead in Cocora (the tiny gateway hamlet to the valley) you'll see vendors offering guided horseback rides, and others renting rubber boots. If you opt to hike, the latter are a must. The main trail includes several river crossings, and although there are rudimentary footbridges, the combination of river waters and damp cloud forests means that sections of the trail can be slick, muddy, or even submerged.

The prime vistas will be accessible to those hikers willing to take on the challenge of a path less traveled: Finca la Montaña. This steep and rocky loop (five to six hours for the whole circuit) begins at the Reserva Natural Acaime trailhead, located on the main road in Cocora, and leads up to fog-shrouded Finca la Montaña, the highest point on the main trail. From here, you walk down into the distinctive groves of slender wax palm trees, and then meander back to Cocora.

From the same trailhead, there is a detour (a shorter up-and-back trek) to the nature reserve at Acaime. Look for the sign indicating the side trail to the Reserva Natural Acaime—it's home to several different kinds of hummingbirds, easily visible at the water feeding stations positioned in the trees. A nominal admission fee to the reserve includes your choice of a hot beverage, including the Andes' favorite *agua de panela* ("panela water"), a tea alternative made from hardened cane sugar.

TRAVELWISE

- **HOW TO VISIT** The closest international airport is El Edén in Armenia, Colombia. From here, take a public bus or taxi to Salento; then hire one of the ubiquitous jeeps to take you to Cocora, jumping-off point for the valley.

- **HOW TO STAY** Breakfast is included at La Serrana Eco Farm and Hostel near Salento. The traditional Colombian hacienda has bunkhouse dorms, private rooms, and optional activities such as horseback riding and coffee plantation tours *(laserrana.com.co)*.

- **PLANNING** Any trail through the valley involves high-altitude hiking. For safety's sake, take a day or two to acclimate to the altitude before attempting either walk *(quindio.travel; colombia.travel/en)*.

Racing below wax palms, national symbol of Colombia and the tallest palm trees in the world

Hikers in the Valle de Cocora brave muddy paths and rickety bridges to get to stunning views.

PICTURE PERFECT

As photographer Alex Treadway approached the Valle de Cocora beneath a blue sky, he could see the giant Quindío wax palms off in the distance. "They're not so impressive from far away," he says. "They actually look small and spindly." But as he walked up the valley, the clouds rolled in and the trees disappeared in the mist. Worried that he wouldn't get a shot at all, he strolled among the palms, and found that the low clouds made them that much more impressive. "[Everything was quiet] except for the gentle swaying and creaking of the impossibly tall trees," he says. "It's a truly atmospheric place."

IMAGE BY ALEX TREADWAY
National Geographic photographer

Colca Canyon

Southern Peru's 60-mile (97 km) Colca Canyon is twice as deep as the Grand Canyon and plunges well over 10,000 feet (3,048 m) to the rapids of Río Colca. In the surrounding valley, hardy locals continue their millennia-old farming practices on terraces of corn, quinoa, and potatoes. Between Spanish colonial towns, alpacas roam, herded by women in voluminous skirts and beribboned hats.

Is it a wonder the Peruvian writer Mario Vargas Llosa called this region the "Valley of Marvels"? At first glance the theatrical landscape of the valley may appear unlikely to support life. The snow-capped peaks of Coropuna and Ampato loom at altitudes over 20,000 feet (6,096 m), and the Andean highland mountainscape leaves you breathless not only from its beauty, but also from thinness of oxygen. The Incas discovered the indigenous communities of the Collagua and Cabana peoples living here in the 15th century, and the Spanish conquistadores came a hundred years later, but this mountainous backwater was largely untouched in modern times until roads arrived in the 1970s.

The Collagua and the Cabana, two distinct ethnic groups, have called this rugged place home since at least 800 B.C., and developed an inventive system of farming that used snowmelt for irrigation, and terraces to prevent erosion. As a result, the Colca Valley's land has yielded crops for millennia, supporting the population of this isolated sliver of land. Today you'll see villages of tin-roofed homes strung together by pebbled roads that snake through the quilted

The Río Colca carved one of the world's deepest canyons (opposite). Nonetheless, this rugged land has long been cultivated; the Quechuan (above) still farm terraced fields of corn and potatoes.

blanket of farmland. Along the way, alpine flowers sprout by the *apachetas,* rocks piled high as tributes to Pachamama, the Mother Earth goddess revered by the indigenous people of the region.

Before the arrival of the 16th-century Spaniards, the Collagua and the Cabana used wood planks and other techniques to cause cranial deformation in order to distinguish members of the two groups. Today, the practice is long discarded in favor of using intricately embroidered hats to differentiate them—and through intermarriage, the two peoples of the Colca Valley have largely united. Their villages are famous throughout Peru for putting on colorful festivals that incorporate traditional dances,

REWIND PILOT, WRITER, EXPLORER

In 1931, historian and writer Robert Shippee (pictured) and photographer George Johnson led an eight-month National Geographic expedition into the then little-known Peruvian interior. They traveled through the remote, precipitous landscape of the Colca Valley on mules, negotiating what Shippee described as "yard-wide, slippery trails that hung in mid-air hundreds of feet above the river."

Shippee was a multitalented adventurer. Not only did he write two *National Geographic* magazine stories on the expedition, he piloted one of the specially designed planes the team used to take aerial photographs of archaeological remnants like the "Great Wall of Peru," a pre-Inca fortification that ribboned for miles over the Andean foothills (Shippee leans on a portion here). So rugged and isolated was the terrain that the team sometimes had to build its own airstrips, a primitive exercise in finding a level stretch of ground and clearing it of boulders. Perhaps it's not surprising that only one of the expedition's planes made it home in one piece, though all the team members did.

music, and Catholic iconography into spirited celebrations.

On the cold and dry higher plains, the people of the Colca Valley have eked out a living by herding alpaca, raised for their tender meat and soft hair, as well as pack llamas that are better suited for the precipitous terrain than horses and donkeys. Also roaming about are families of vicuña, members of the camel family and untamed cousins to the llama.

The Colca Valley is also an unexpected mecca for bird-watchers. Even in Peru, which boasts about 1,800 bird species, the Colca region is a particularly excellent place to spot winged creatures like eagles and giant hummingbirds. The undisputed queen of the Colca Valley heavens is the Andean condor, which rides thermal currents across blue skies, rarely flapping its intimidating wings.

The Church of Santa Ana in the small village of Maca is a legacy of the Spanish 16th-century conquest of the region.

Considered sacred by the Incas and ranking as one of the world's largest flying creatures, the condors can stand 4 feet (1.2 m) high and have wingspans of 10 feet (3 m). This endangered species has become one of the Colca Valley's great attractions, and visitors flock to the popular tourist viewpoint of Cruz del Cóndor to see the massive raptors cruise.

For more intrepid visitors, Río Colca has about 300 rapids that attract experienced rafters. On foot, you can trek for a day or many days along the canyon's rim, or descend thousands of feet between the far-flung villages of the valley.

▶ TRAVELWISE

• **HOW TO VISIT** Chivay, 100 miles (161 km) from the city Arequipa, is the valley's regional hub, where you can make tour arrangements. The climate is generally cool and dry. November through March has the driest, sunniest weather. Visitors are legally required to purchase a tourist ticket of 70 soles (around $20) that helps finance infrastructure like roads.

• **PLANNING** The official tourism office of Peru has info in English (*peru.travel*); Colca region's official website is in Spanish (*colcaperu.gob.pe*).

• **HOW TO STAY** The 20-cabin Las Casitas del Colca (*lascasitasdelcolca.com*) is the area's most luxurious accommodation, and is located in the heart of the canyon.

PICTURE PERFECT

Wild vicuña are corralled near the remote southern Peru village of Picotani during Gran Chaccu, the annual shearing roundup rooted in Incan tradition. Photographer Beth Wald recalls how, on the day of the event, Quechua villagers from surrounding communities turned up, mostly on foot. "Women started cooking, musicians arrived . . . and there were traditional dances and other ceremonies." Getting photos of the vicuña was a physically challenging assignment. "The chaccu took place at close to 15,000 feet," Wald says, "and I had to try to keep up with the local people who were herding the vicuña . . . they moved very fast up and down the hills looking for the animals."

IMAGE BY BETH WALD
National Geographic photographer

Moon Valley

Located just 6 miles (10 km) from the center of La Paz in Bolivia, the Valle de la Luna, or "Valley of the Moon," does indeed feel like the terrain of a celestial body. The wrinkled, arid landscape is made up of ragged pinnacles of soft clay and sandstone, remnants of mountains worn away by rain and wind. The hues and shadows of this desertscape shift with the passing of the sun.

Many places all over the world are called Valley of the Moon, including neighboring Argentina's stark, wind- and water-eroded rock formations at the edge of the Andes. The Valley of the Moon in Bolivia supposedly received its name from no more scientific a source than American astronaut Neil Armstrong, who upon seeing it remarked how much it reminded him of his lunar visit in 1969.

This vista is primarily one of gray and tan peaks, with intermittent crimson and violet towers. Cactus and a few hardy flowering plants peep between stone spires. Two different paths break through the small valley, which reminds some visitors of Utah's hoodoo-strewn Bryce Canyon. One route is a mere 15-minute walk along a clearly marked trail. The longer route takes just under an hour, and brings you to the top of Muela del Diablo, or "Devil's Tooth." This extinct volcano looks like a cracked, diabolical tooth and rises about 500 feet (152 m) above the surrounding landscape. From its summit, you can see Bolivia's capital city La Paz and the entire valley and its rippling badlands spread out before you.

Bolivia's Valley of the Moon is a cluster of tall, weathered rock pinnacles that are the last remaining bits of mountains (opposite). The nearby Tiwanaku ruins harbor relics like this pre-Columbian statue (above).

Make sure you bring water and wear sunscreen on any excursion in this high-altitude, dry locale. The sun is strong, and chances to refill your water bottle are scarce once you venture into the valley. Be respectful of the landscape, too—though the valley is a protected site, the adjacent small town of Mallasa is slowly spreading, increasing the threat of erosion to the soft soil.

If you're up for a side trip after a trek through Valley of the Moon, the ruins of Tiwanaku, a UNESCO World Heritage site, are just over an hour and a half away. This city was the capital of the Tiwanaku Empire, a pre-Columbian civilization that lasted some 3,000 years and predated the Inca expansion into the region. Highlights of this archaeological site include various temples, the massive, megalithic stone arch called Gate of the Sun, a pyramid, and partially reconstructed walls that once surrounded the city.

The vivid colors of local weavings stand out at an evening market in La Paz (above); the stark beauty of Valley of the Moon, just a few miles away, is a much more monochrome spectacle (opposite).

TRAVELWISE

- **HOW TO VISIT** Valley of the Moon's proximity to La Paz makes it easy to visit; various local tour companies offer excursions. Local buses or taxis can also make the trip to the valley within 40 minutes, allowing you to wander at your own pace.

- **PLANNING** The Vice Ministry of Tourism runs a good website for planning travel and excursions in the country (*bolivia.travel*).

- **HOW TO STAY** You'll have no trouble finding lodging in La Paz—the city has hostels, budget hotels, and luxury accommodations. If you want to get out of La Paz, Colibri Camping and Eco Lodge is just five minutes from Mallasa and is a more rustic experience (*colibricamping.com*).

Alberto de Agostini

There aren't many places left that truly look like pristine Earth, but this vast reserve at the bottom of South America exudes that rugged canvas. A mélange of forests, glaciers and snowcapped peaks, lagoons, and oceanic straits, Agostini remains largely unexplored. And given the region's remoteness, extreme geography, and harsh weather, it will likely remain that way for generations.

Alberto de Agostini National Park was founded in 1965 and was named after an Italian missionary turned explorer. Born and raised in northern Italy, Alberto de Agostini was dispatched to southern Chile in 1910 to attend to the spiritual needs of the few remaining Patagonian Indians. A true renaissance man, Father de Agostini combined his missionary work with mountain climbing, trekking, writing, photography, filmmaking, geology, and ethnology. Over the next 50 years he penned 22 books on the region, describing places few men had stepped before him.

Today, the park protects the western extreme of Tierra del Fuego and smaller islands, many of them never inhabited. With a land area of more than 5,600 square miles (14,504 sq km), it is larger than Yellowstone and Yosemite combined, and just as rich in geography and wildlife. Animals in the park are abundant and unperturbed by human presence, from marine-dwelling whales, seals, and penguins to foxes, guanaco, condors, and millions of seabirds. Among the best places to spot larger animals are the small island at the mouth of Ainsworth Bay (elephant seals) and the

Stirred by unpredictable winds, the waters of the Strait of Magellan lap the rocky coastline of the Tierra del Fuego (opposite). The archipelago is home to the Magellanic woodpecker (above), known for its coloring and reverberating "toc toc toc" pecks.

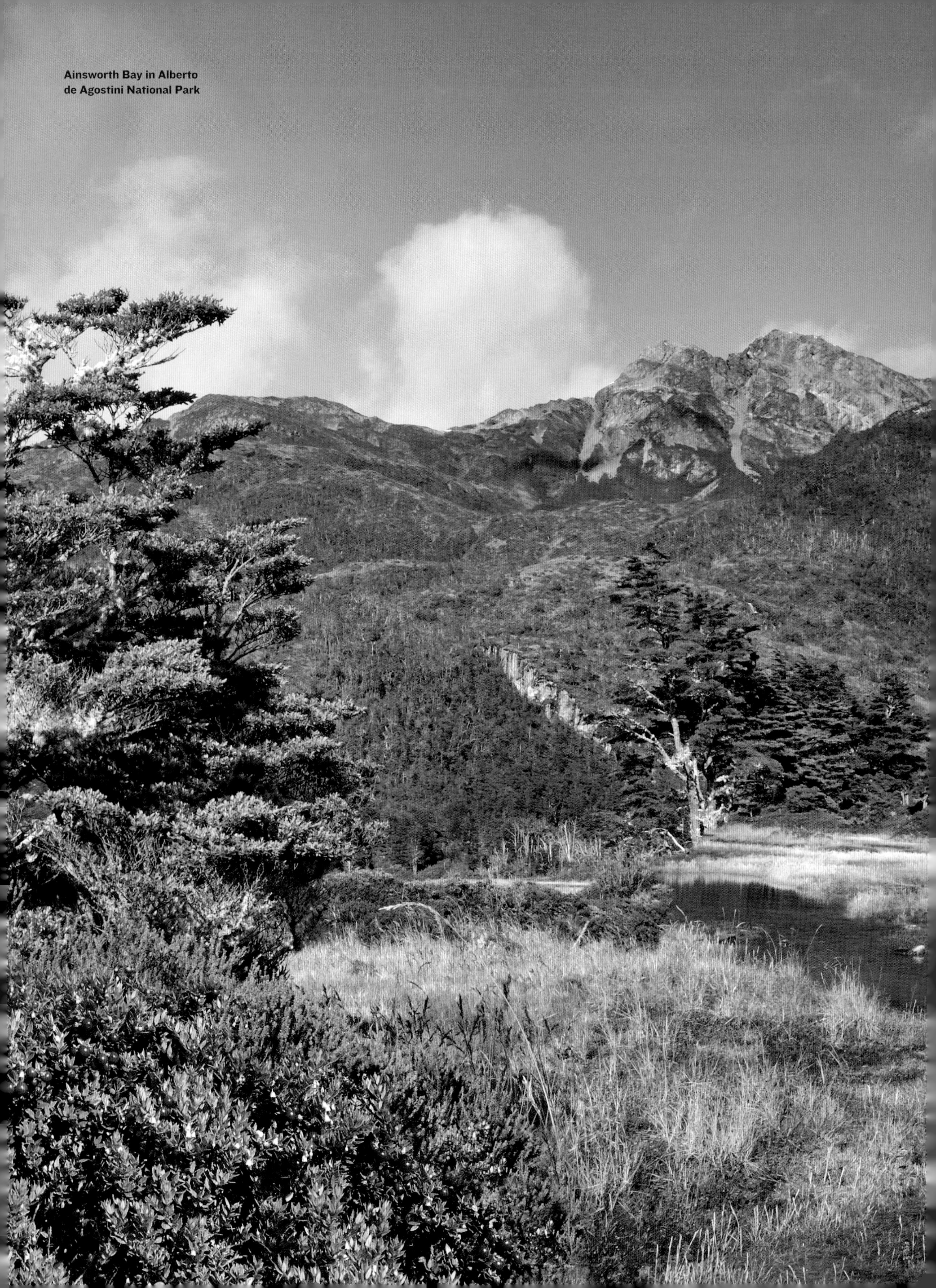

Ainsworth Bay in Alberto de Agostini National Park

terminal end of Parry Fjord (leopard seals). And despite its name, Aguila ("Eagle") Glacier is actually a great place to spot condors, hovering in the updrafts or perched on lofty rocks around the glacier's mirrorlike lagoon.

One of the most revealing facts about Agostini is that there are no roads into the park. Likewise, there are no airstrips (although a floatplane would be an excellent way to explore the region). Most of the several thousand people who visit the park each year arrive on small expedition cruise ships sailing from Punta Arenas, Chile, or Ushuaia, Argentina. Likewise, there are no hotels, lodges, or organized campsites inside the park. Those who wish to stay overnight are on their own.

Many of Agostini's landmarks are arrayed along the south side of Seno Almirantazgo (Admiralty Sound). Ainsworth Bay is a microcosm of what makes this park so special: A mosaic of sandy strands, delicate peat bogs, and thick Magellanic woodland flush with native coigüe trees, all set against a backdrop of Marinelli Glacier inching down from the massive Darwin Icefield. Nearby Brookes Bay occupies a classic U-shaped glacial valley, a spectacular fjord that ends in a black-sand beach that curves around the shore to the base of Brookes Glacier. Calving off the glacier, icebergs float across the bay and eventually wash up onto the beach like abstract ice sculptures amid the driftwood.

The legendary Beagle Channel slices through the middle of

Three explorers in red coats give some scale
to the massive Agostini Glacier.

Still rugged and unexplored to this day, Alberto de Agostini wasn't even yet a national park when the *National Geographic* husband/wife team Jean and Franc Shor traveled through Argentina in 1957 and 1958 and headed down to the remote reaches of Tierra del Fuego. At that point, getting to Ushuaia—the "southernmost town in the world," near the tip of South America—was a challenging prospect indeed. The Shors hired a plucky taxi driver and his cab, and managed to get across the stormy Strait of Magellan on a World War II landing craft that had been converted into a ferry.

However, they found they had actually preceded the completion of the very first road being built to Ushuaia. To get through the Garibaldi Pass and the snowcapped Martial Mountains, the Shors and their taxi had to be towed behind the bulldozer actually *building* this first access road (pictured). Prior to this, Ushuaia had been reached by boat or plane.

range of the Andes before they finally peter out in the jigsaw puzzle of islands around Cape Horn. And being Andes, they are quite impressive, more than half a dozen peaks more than 6,000 feet (1,828 m) high, including several that seem to rise straight from the sea. Among the more prominent are needlelike Mount Buckland (5,728 ft/1,746 m) and a giant pyramid called Mount Sarmiento (7,369 ft/2,246 m). Father de Agostini was obsessed with the latter, and though he tried several times, he never reached the summit.

TRAVELWISE

- **HOW TO VISIT** The only way to reach the park is by private boat or small expedition cruise ships, which only venture into Agostini during the Southern Hemisphere summer (late September to early April). Even then, weather is highly changeable.

- **PLANNING** Tierra del Fuego is remote and lightly visited. Turismo Chile has info on what to see and do in the country (*visit.chile.travel*).

- **HOW TO STAY** Agostini National Park offers no land-based accommodation. Australis cruises (*australis.com*) operates round-trip voyages into park waters from Punta Arenas (Chile) and journeys between Ushuaia (Argentina) and Punta Arenas.

Agostini, and splits into two watery arms that embrace the Isla Gordon. It was along this channel, aboard the H.M.S. *Beagle*, that Charles Darwin saw his first glaciers in 1833. It was clearly a jaw-dropping encounter, for the famed naturalist was inspired to write in his journal: "It is scarcely possible to imagine anything more beautiful than the beryl-like blue of these glaciers, and especially as contrasted with the dead white of the upper expanse of snow."

Beagle Channel and Admiralty Sound are separated by a knot of mountains called the Cordillera Darwin—the southernmost

PICTURE
PERFECT

Cowboys—called *bagualeros*—round up their horses on a peaceful Tierra del Fuego evening. "The Chilean side of Tierra del Fuego is one of the wildest places I've seen," says photographer Tomás Munita, who followed a group of bagualeros as they trapped wild horses for *estancia* (ranch) work. "We spent every single day riding horses through the incredible *lenga* forests. It was just the sound of the branches breaking under our horses' hoofs, an occasional guanaco alerting other animals of our presence, and birds. The rest was silence and the intensity of the eyes of the cowboys tracking their prey."

IMAGE BY TOMÁS MUNITA
National Geographic photographer

Jujuy Province

Jujuy Province in northwest Argentina is the country's interface with the desert: a land remote, arid, and dramatically handsome, with rock-walled canyons, towering cardon cactus, and whitewashed mission churches. An ever changing palette of light, shadow, and color transforms Jujuy into a photographer's paradise . . . or simply an incredible country to be savored with the naked eye.

Located in the rain shadow of the Andes, Jujuy Province sees scant precipitation even in the best of years. And although it's not quite as dry as the Atacama of northern Chile or the vast salt pans of southern Bolivia, the province's high-altitude *Puna* ("grassland") landscapes are strewn with *salinas* ("salt plains"), sandy arroyos, and treeless peaks. The beauty is in the detail: flocks of pink flamingos on shallow lakes, canyons with secluded waterfalls, and mountains that turn a majestic purple as the sun sinks behind the Andes in late afternoon.

Founded in 1593 as a stopover on the route to the Spanish silver mines in Bolivia, San Salvador de Jujuy (pronounced *hoo-hooey*) is the province's small but amiable capital and a convenient base for exploring the region's natural wonders. North of the city, Highway 9 meanders up the Rio Grande and the famed Quebrada de Humahuaca, a nearly 100-mile-long (161 km) valley between the towns of Volcán and Tres Cruces, designated a UNESCO World Heritage site because of its outstanding scenery and cultural heritage.

In the Jujuy desert, the hues and textures of the rolling landscape are phenomena of geology and the elements (opposite).
Brighter yet are the colors of the region's llama and alpaca wool textiles (above), often sold at local markets.

In a desert basin, the salt flats of Salinas Grandes are mined through rectangular pools.

In 1957–1958, *National Geographic* staffers Jean and Franc Shor navigated great stretches of northern and southern Argentina by plane, steamboat, and taxi, and co-authored an account of this adventure in the March 1958 edition of the magazine. Arriving in balmy San Salvador de Jujuy at midnight on Christmas Eve, the Shors watched thousands of townspeople gather near its central cathedral for a dazzling, alfresco Catholic service. "On the hills behind the cathedral, people were shooting fireworks, and the skyrockets arched against the stars, bursting brightly above the soaring flood-lighted towers," the Shors related.

The following day, from the verdant lawn of the Hotel Altos de la Viña, overlooking the Rio Grande, they enjoyed the upbeat dances of a folk group (pictured), set to the music of flutes, drums, and guitars. The group specialized in the traditional dances of the Jujuy Province, and the Shors thought them rather akin to the gambols of North American square dancers.

The drive north leads through intriguing terrain. The Cerro de los Siete Colores (Hill of Seven Colors) rises just west of Purmamarca village. As the name suggests, the geological oddity flaunts seven different hues ranging from red, purple, and pink to beige, khaki, and brown. Geologists say the effervescent colors derive from sediments deposited by the sea, lakes, and rivers over millions of years.

A similar spectacle unfolds another 43 miles (69 km) up the Rio Grande on the outskirts of Humahuaca village, where the saw-toothed Serranía del Hornocal mountains flash an even greater array of earthy colors created by the same geological forces. Locals claim you can count 33 different hues in the stone. After crossing a bridge, Highway 73 winds upward about 15 miles (24 km) to the start of a trail with incredible views of the triangular formations.

All of the Quebrada villages boast a large indigenous population, residents who trace their roots to the ancient Andes rather than Iberia. The valley's cultural patrimony is most evident in the town Tilcara, home to an ancient stone citadel called Pucará de Tilcara. Partially rebuilt in modern times, this Argentine national monument was originally erected by the Omaguaca people at least 800 years ago.

From Purmamarca, Highway 52 climbs out of the Quebrada and over the mountains via a lofty pass called Cuesta del Lipán (also dubbed the "Door to the Andes"). The behemoth mountains, a line of snowcapped peaks and volcanoes on the western horizon, can be seen from the pass's 13,680-foot (4,170 m) summit. Argentina's most spectacular highway then plunges down dozens of hairpins to a desert basin that harbors another of Jujuy's natural wonders—Salinas Grandes. The one-time lake evaporated after the last ice age, leaving an enormous, bone-dry salt flat around the size of Chicago.

Farther north on the *altiplano* ("high plain"), Laguna de los Pozuelos gives a hint at what Salinas Grandes must have been like before it went dry. Filled with brackish water, the lake supports a wide variety of avian life, including three flamingo species that

Small villages dot the red- and orange-tinted canyon
known as the Quebrada de Humahuaca.

nest in its shallow waters. Andean condors and flightless rheas also frequent the area.

But the province isn't all desert. Eastern Jujuy is a world of fertile river valleys and remote mountains wrapped in a thick neotropical forest the locals call *Yungas*. The steep mountains and deep valleys of Calilegua National Park preserve the largest and most accessible yungas. Among the animals that roam beneath the park's ubiquitous Andean alders and mountain pines are jaguars, pumas, and tapir. Accessed from the town of Calilegua, the park offers hiking trails and primitive camping with hardly another soul around.

TRAVELWISE

• **HOW TO VISIT** The drive from Buenos Aires to Jujuy is nearly a thousand miles (1,609 km); flight time from BA is two hours. Good roads and scant traffic make the province perfect for a self-drive; rental cars are available in San Salvador de Jujuy. Local outfitters like Diungo Tours in Tilcara offer guided trips *(diungo.com;* Spanish*)*. Caravana de Llamas organizes llama day tours in the Quebrada *(caravanadellamas.com.ar)*.

• **PLANNING** Argentina Tourist Board offers general information on traveling in the country *(argentina.travel/en)*.

• **HOW TO STAY** Tilcara has emerged as the hip place to stay in the Quebrada. Accommodation ranges from budget hostels to the sleek Las Marías Hotel Boutique *(lasmariastilcara.com.ar/en/home)*.

PICTURE
PERFECT

When photographer Marco Verna-schi visited Argentina's isolated region of Jujuy to explore its cultural diversity, he was tired of pictures depicting the region's farmers as digging in the dirt. "I wanted to portray them differently," he once said. "I chose to focus on their cultures. That's why I asked the Suri girl . . . to dress in traditional ceremonial apparel for [her] portrait." He remembers how a strong wind started blowing during the shoot. "The feathers of the costume were flying everywhere. In the end, however, the wind helped create the photograph's mystery, with the feathers partially covering her face."

IMAGE BY MARCO VERNASCHI
National Geographic contributing
photographer

A boardwalk leads through
the beauty of Plitvice Lakes
in Croatia.

Europe

Even the long-settled continent of Europe has rugged corners
—Iceland's highlands, the wind-tossed Faroe Islands,
and in Poland, a primeval forest where bison still roam.

Landmannalaugar Rhyolite Mountains

The colorful lava fields and rhyolite mountains of Fjallabak Nature Reserve in the highlands of Iceland are truly an awesome sight. This marbled, crumpled landscape was created when southern Iceland's volcanoes belched forth thick rhyolite lava that flowed and cooled slowly. Billowing white steam venting from below the earth is a reminder that this region still is not at rest.

The mountainous area of Landmannalaugar is the crown jewel of Fjallabak Nature Reserve. Here, in the heart of the reserve, the undulating mountains seem to have been rendered by a crazed, skillful hand. Streaks of pink, yellow, and blue paint the slopes, interspersed with vivid tongues of orange and brown. Contrasting with these fiery hues are low-growing, bright green fields of cotton grass that reach up the mountains and down into the valleys. Rhyolite lava can cool quickly, and when it does, it hardens into glassy, black obsidian, like the kind you'll see strewn across the Laugahraun lava field, a pitted moonscape at the base of the mountains.

For the most dazzling experience of Landmannalaugar, cross your fingers for a sunny day—but know that most days are not. If you camp in the reserve, you'll get a whole different perspective on this remote northern world. After sunset at the end of the season, when the nights get truly dark, the colorful rhyolite mountains are swallowed by blackness and you're treated to another wild, distant frontier: the spectacular starry sky.

Water braids its way through the multicolored mountains and valleys of Landmannalaugar (opposite), where visitors can soak in geothermal hot springs (above).

A visitor regards a terrain of vivid colors, created by the activity of the nearby volcano Hekla.

leads up Mount Bláhnúkur—the "blue peak"—with beautiful views of the reserve. Veteran hikers backpack the whole of the Laugavegur hiking trail, a multiday, 34-mile (55-km) route that connects Landmannalaugar and the valley of Þórsmörk to the south.

Perhaps the most photographed of all of the region's memorable sites is the Ljótipollur explosion crater—literally the "ugly puddle," though it's anything but. The crater is filled with a deep blue lake that is cupped by steep red and green walls hundreds of feet tall. If you are a fisherman, you'll find further riches in the lake's abundant brown trout population.

For all of the Landmannalaugar's rough, rugged beauty, there is a serenity here, too, beside the Ljótipollur crater and along the blue rivers that meander through canyons carpeted with wild grasses and tiny white wild flowers. After a vigorous hike, it is a treat to realize that those rivers are in fact fed by hot springs. There may be no more satisfying way to take in the splendor of Landmannalaugar than to recline in the warm waters and gaze up.

The rocky roads that lead to the Fjallabak Nature Reserve are themselves an adventure—they are accessible in the summer months, but then only by four-wheel-drive. The most popular route, F208, approaches from the north and travels along (and sometimes through) the region's rivers.

Sturdy hiking boots are a must for exploring the Landmannalaugar's varied terrain. A well-traveled two-hour loop takes you through the Laugahraun lava field into the Grænagil gorge and on to Mount Brennisteinsalda, an active volcano and possibly the region's most colorful mountain. Black obsidian, blue lava, green mosses, and red iron all contribute to the spectrum of colors splashed over its slopes. Here too are unmistakable indicators that subsurface activity is afoot—mud pools and vents release plumes of noxious-smelling sulfur into the air. Another, much steeper path

REWIND AN UNDERGROUND OVEN

This photo from National Geographic's archive was shot in 1941 in Iceland, but is otherwise scant on details. It does identify the boy, Sonny, who is hard at work at an unusual chore. The caption reads, "Sonny goes out to see if the bread is cooked well. Placed in a bucket, the dough is baked to a crisp brown by the boiling underground heating system in the land of no fuel."

The volcanic power simmering beneath Iceland's surface has tremendous capabilities for geothermal heat, and by the 20th century, Icelanders had long been making direct use of it for bathing and baking. The "hot spring bread" Sonny watches over is called *hverabrauð*, and the islanders had probably been baking it for centuries. Though geothermal energy is now harnessed on a much larger scale, Icelanders still bake hot spring bread, a rye called *rúgbrauð* that's sealed in a pot and simmered underground for 12 to 24 hours.

The volcanic crater of Ljótípollur steams vigorously, a reminder of the power just under Earth's crust.

PICTURE
PERFECT

A geomagnetic storm lights up the evening twilight above Iceland's iconic Kirkjufell glacier. "A good image doesn't usually happen by pure luck," says photographer Babak Tafreshi. "Studying the phenomenon and the location is key." He had been shooting in Iceland when he noticed a major flaring sunspot on the Earth-facing side of the sun, with the potential to ignite a coronal mass ejection. "I had a couple days until the particles would reach the Earth's magnetic field and create a massive aurora display." When it came, he was ready.

IMAGE BY BABAK TAFRESHI
National Geographic photographer

DENMARK

Faroe Islands

In the mighty swells of the wild North Atlantic, about 200 miles (322 km) off the coast of Scotland, sits a misty archipelago of 18 islands and hundreds of islets and skerries. These are the Faroe Islands, windblown and remote, with all the antiquity and modernity of their Danish motherland. They are home to rugged mountains and green, treeless slopes that suddenly drop thousands of feet into craggy fjords.

The Faroes possess a rich human heritage dating back to the fourth through sixth centuries, when historians think Irish or Scottish monks may have lived on the islands. Those communities were overrun and largely destroyed by a ninth-century Viking invasion, so little evidence of that era remains. Today the islands (17 of them are populated by about 50,000 total inhabitants) are marked by bright, colorful cottages and turf-roofed wooden churches that bring a cozy human presence to these brooding, primordial moorlands. A labyrinth of walking paths traverse vertigo-inducing cliffs, while winding roads and subsea tunnels connect the islands both aboveground and below sea level. The islanders themselves are a hardy, taciturn group with their own language, Faroese, that exhibits many qualities of Old Norse and is closely related to Icelandic.

The king of these salty islands is Streymoy, the largest and easily the most scenic of the archipelago. It is home to the buzzy, arty, and food-forward capital Tórshavn. More natural wonders like bird cliffs over 1,500 feet (457 m) and sea grottoes are found near

In spring, verdant green blankets the rocky slopes of the Faroe Islands, where sheer cliffs rise and fall steeply into the North Atlantic (opposite and above). This isolated archipelago between Norway and Iceland is home to 50,000 people.

The lighthouse on Mykines Holm flashes about every seven seconds, and is tethered with guy wires to stabilize it in relentless winds.

the town of Vestmanna, on the west side of the island, and these are best experienced during a sunny summer boat excursion.

The six Northern Islands—Borðoy, Kunoy, Kalsoy, Viðoy, Svínoy, and Fugloy—offer the most dramatic landscape and best demonstrate the Faroes' fiery volcanic origins. This era of volcanism, 60 million years ago, left behind layers of basalt that eventually cropped up to form the dramatic sea islands and cliffs you see today. There are no active volcanoes left in the Faroe Islands now, but the abrupt outcrops, rippled cones, and angular, upthrust landforms of the archipelago are evidence of the eruptions millions of years ago. The Southern Islands—Suðuroy, Skúvoy, and sand dune–lined Sandoy—have less theatrical landscape, but offer a chance to explore small rustic villages and hiking trails that

cross moorland, peat bogs, and several important birding areas.

With almost 700 miles (1,127 km) of coastline, these islands are a seabird lover's mecca. The species include puffins, skuas, guillemots, and fulmars that make the most of the Gulf Stream–warmed waters, and fill the air with haunting cries that add a melancholic quality to an already lonely landscape.

Today's travelers would be remiss to not also spend time getting to know the rich culture of the Faroe Islands. The islanders have carried their centuries-old folk heritage into the modern age with everything from lace knitwear to controversial whaling festivals. One of the best expressions of this folk culture is the islanders' vibrant tradition of music, which includes everything from medieval ballads to modern indie. Although the Faroese have a rich

Brightly colored boat hulls and houses welcome visitors to Tórshavn, the largest town on the Faroe Islands.

Writer and photographer Leo Hansen made over 200 boat trips in the North Atlantic for his photographic survey of the Faroe Islands, published in *National Geographic* magazine in 1930. He traveled in a Viking-style boat called *Tusk* that had once been propelled by 10 oars, but had been converted with a motor for his purposes. Hansen ventured from his base in Tórshavn to many outlying islands, capturing hardy Viking descendants as they eked out an existence on the remote archipelago.

He was taken with the Faroes' self-sustaining, scrappy residents, but aghast at their cuisine—pulverized dried salt fish, skinned sheep cured for a year and then eaten raw, month-seasoned whale blubber, and cured seabird. In this wharf-side photograph, women scrubbed fresh codfish, readying it for the drying process. Whole communities participated in this chore, spreading filets along shorelines or on racks, shooing away seabirds, and gathering everything up at the first sign of squalls—sometimes seven times a day.

adventurous, eclectic eaters can try Faroese delicacies like the wind-dried and salted flesh of fish, seabirds, and sheep; cured or fermented pilot whale meat; or sheep sausage. Diners around the world are increasingly seeking seafood like cod, salmon, shellfish, and lobster caught in the pristine waters offshore.

TRAVELWISE

- **HOW TO VISIT** There is one airport serving the Faroe Islands, located on the island of Vágar and connected to the capital city Tórshavn on Streymoy by a subsea tunnel. Atlantic Airways is the only airline that serves the Faroes by regular commercial service. The islands are also served by year-round ferry from Denmark, which takes 36 hours (*atlantic.fo; smyrilline.com*).

- **PLANNING** A couple good websites are full of trail and birding information as well as cultural and historical info, and even music festival listings for Tórshavn (*faroeislands.com; visitfaroeislands.com*).

- **HOW TO STAY** The charming turf-roofed Gjáargarður Guesthouse is located in the village of Gjógv, on Eysturoy. The 14-room wooden hotel offers sightings of puffins and views of the cliffs in Ambadalur Valley (*gjaargardur.fo*).

history of oral storytelling and a tradition of literature that goes all the way back to 13th-century sagas written by Icelanders, it was only in the 19th century that they began writing themselves, and they have made up for lost time by penning a rich selection of crime fiction, poetry, and children's literature.

In recent years, a new kind of visitor has been arriving in the Faroes: the foodie. Long before foraging became a trendy concept and New Nordic cuisine swept the streets and kitchens of Copenhagen, the Faroese had been making use of locally foraged plants like nettles, seaweed, scurvy grass, and angelica. More

PICTURE
PERFECT

On Denmark's Faroese island of Streymoy, a grass-roofed Saksun village is tucked away at the bottom of a mountain-enclosed inlet of the sea. Photographer Karine Aigner came to this mystical, moody realm for a photo shoot with a famous Faroese chef. "As a photographer you need to deal with mist, fog, wind, and rain," she says. "I had to set up strobes and a soft box, and it started to rain, and the wind kept picking up the soft box and flying it across the edge of the lake." Her take-away? "Sometimes the elements make for very interesting images."

IMAGE BY KARINE AIGNER
National Geographic photographer

Skellig Islands

Locals call them "the rocks." But that austere name belies the ghostly beauty of these two sea-lapped volcanic islands. Jutting from the stormy Atlantic Ocean like a pair of sunken Gothic spires, the jagged salt-encrusted islands sit just 7.5 miles (12 km) off Ireland's Iveragh Peninsula, but remain a world apart. Little Skellig prohibits people altogether, and Skellig Michael permits limited visitation.

In around the sixth century, Skellig Michael was home to Christian monks who carved steps into its volcanic and red sandstone, and lived on little more than collected rainwater, seabird eggs, and their faith. These ascetic monks occupied tiny clocháns—beehive-shaped stone huts—for up to 600 years, enduring storms, Viking attacks, and at times, famine. The islands are not just a sacred and mystical site, but are also a testament to human grit and survival.

Skellig Michael's six corbel-style beehive cells, two oratories, and dozens of lichen-encrusted slab crosses are centuries old, but most are in pristine condition. These structures have been unoccupied since the monks abandoned Skellig Michael in the 13th century, probably because of worsening climactic conditions and changes in the structure of the church in Ireland.

Most scholars agree that Skellig Michael was uninhabited prior to the residency of the monks, though Irish folklore claims that Ir, son of Míl Espáine (a folkloric figure in Irish history who was father of the nation's founding race), was buried on the rocky Atlantic islet around 1400 B.C. after he drowned in a shipwreck.

Accessible only by boat in fair weather, the Skellig Islands (opposite) are summer home to thousands of Atlantic puffins (above), which compete for nest space on these rocky crags off the southwestern coast of Ireland.

In the rock of Skellig Michael, 618 steep steps (above) remain of those the Christian monks once carved. The island can be reached from the cheerful harbor town of Portmagee (opposite).

Though uninhabited by humans today, the islands are an important home to several seabird colonies, including puffins and fulmars, whose haunting cries fill the cold, salty air.

Getting to the Skellig Islands is no small feat. It requires a one-hour ferry crossing from harbors on the mainland like Portmagee and Ballinskelligs. The ferries only set forth in ideal (and rare) weather conditions—swells and drizzle are frequent, and boat captains won't transport visitors when the seas are rough.

If you're lucky enough to book a ferry and keep the date, the best view of the Skelligs is during the approach by boat. The dark, eerie islands appear to float on the choppy ocean surrounding them, and the effect is hypnotic. Too many visitors witness the islands through the screens of their smartphones—be sure to spend time gazing at these isolated, ancient Atlantic islands with the naked eye, as it's an experience you likely won't get again.

TRAVELWISE

• **HOW TO VISIT** The closest international airport is Shannon Airport, three hours from Portmagee. Tour operators like Casey's Skellig Islands Tours (*skelligislands.com*) run boat trips to Skellig Michael April to Oct.

• **PLANNING** The Tourism Ireland website is a good resource for travelers (*ireland.com*), while Casey's Boat Trips runs a helpful site with info on the history of the island, its bird life, and links to other planning resources (*skelligislands.com*).

• **HOW TO STAY** A joint Lindblad Expeditions-National Geographic tour offers a cruise of the Irish Isles, including a day to explore the Skellig Islands and the Dingle Peninsula (*expeditions.com*).

Volcans d'Auvergne

A chain of slumbering volcanoes called Chaîne des Puys, rounded and velvet green, slinks across central France's Massif Central to create one of the most stunning, distinctive landscapes in western Europe. Given the tranquility and beauty of the terrain today, it's difficult to imagine that some 65 million years ago, it was in fiery upheaval—one of the world's greatest cradles of volcanism.

From a visitor's point of view, the scenery created by this geological phenomena is breathtaking, a landscape pocked with huge craters and rippled by volcanic peaks, interspersed with glistening lakes and soft-green meadows. From a geologist's perspective, it's a fascinating study in geography and volcanism: The whole area comprises one of France's most tectonically unstable areas, the San Andreas Fault of the French mainland. Established in 1977, the Parc Naturel Régional des Volcans d'Auvergne—France's largest regional park, at more than 976,066 acres (395,000 ha)—was established to preserve this realm of (scientists hope) dormant geological fury.

Some credit French geologist Jean Étienne Guettard with discovering Auvergne's volcanism in the 1700s, but not much was known about these volcanoes until the 1820s, when English geologist George Scrope studied the region and published a tome that essentially laid the foundation for the scientific principles of basic volcanology.

The park's centerpiece is the famed lava dome Puy de Dôme, near

In the Parc Naturel Régional des Volcans d'Auvergne, summertime brings long-horned Salers cows to graze at high altitudes in the Sancy Mountains (above). As the days grow shorter, russet leaves blow around woods and waterfalls and mark the approach of winter (opposite).

The steep, mountainous country of the Parc Naturel Régional des Volcans d'Auvergne makes it a popular locale for winter sports.

the city of Clermont-Ferrand. The oldest and highest volcano in the Chaîne des Puys, it soars 4,803 feet (1,464 m) above the land, its dramatic cone shape the result of its relative newness—it erupted "only" about 7,775 years ago. From the windblown summit, accessible via precipitous road, rack railway, or ancient Roman track, breathtaking views span almost an eighth of France on a rare clear day. Certainly the rest of the Chaîne des Puys is visible, with 80-some cinder cones, lava domes, explosion craters, and maars (broad, low craters). As wispy clouds tickle distant peaks and cast shadows across the landscape far below, it's easy to see why the summit has been considered mystical since prehistoric times. The remnants of the Gallo-Roman temple of Mercury, built of lava stone and marble, is just below the summit and gives credence to this age-old sense of sanctity.

To the southwest of Puy de Dôme, in the heart of the park, three giant volcanoes and their attendant peaks comprise the Massif du Sancy, a heavily wooded mountainscape crisscrossed with ice-cold rivers, sparkling lakes, and hiking trails—you could very well call this region France's lake district. The massif's tallest peak, Puy de Sancy, rises 6,187 feet (1,886 m) above the surrounding landscape. Visitors take a combo of shuttle and cable car from the town of Le Mont-Dore up the peak, and then make a long hike to the summit. Two other giant volcanoes—Banne d'Ordanche and Puy de l'Aiguiller—complete the trio.

Farther south, the Monts du Cantal comprises the vestiges of Europe's largest stratovolcano (with a diameter of 43 miles/69 km). Imploding nine million years ago and again six million years

It had a volatile past, but the dormant volcano **Puy de Dôme** is peaceful and green today, and topped by the ruins of a Roman temple.

In around 1966, *National Geographic*'s assistant editor Kenneth MacLeish embarked on a journey through France to trace the course of the Loire River, and the history that had been laid along its banks over centuries. In Le Puy, in the Auvergne region, MacLeish parked his car overnight in a quiet square. He woke the next morning to find it inaccessible in the midst of market-day clamor, and adorned with a parking ticket. "I found it . . . buried in a frantic melee of carts, quacks, curses, bleats, bellows, and the full-throated soprano protest of pigs being hoisted by an ear and a tail. I had gotten myself a ticket and an audience," MacLeish wrote.

This was Le Puy's chaotic, cheerful Saturday market (pictured), and the townspeople were quite anxious for MacLeish and his offending car to be off. It took a policeman to help him extract the vehicle from the teeming square. "I drove off," MacLeish noted wryly, "in a blue haze of friendly obscenity."

hams and dried sausages are local specialties, and the hamlet Le-Puy-en-Velay is famed for its prized green lentils, best stewed with slivers of pork. Auvergne's Route des Fromages (Cheese Trail) is a chance to sample the famous bleu d'Auvergne, and one of France's oldest cheeses, Fourme d'Ambert.

▶ TRAVELWISE

• **HOW TO VISIT** The closest airport is Clermont-Ferrand, the Auvergne's largest city. A year-round destination, the park covers more than 75 miles (121 km) north to south, with altitudes ranging from 1,312 to 6,188 feet (400 to 1,886 m). Most visitors base themselves conveniently to the Puy-de-Dôme region; the other districts are more remote.

• **PLANNING** Several sites have info on the region and visiting (*auvergne-tourism.com; auvergne-sancy.com; france-voyage.com; campingfrance.com*).

• **HOW TO STAY** The stone village of Orcival, the spa town of Le Mont-Dore, and the lakeside village of Aydat all have good options for hotels, B&Bs, and gîtes (holiday rentals). Visit the park's website for more guidance and info about camping (*www.parcdesvolcans.fr*).

ago, the remaining caldera was then shaved and smoothed by Ice Age glaciers, leaving behind today's undulating landscape scattered with a series of plateaus, beautiful cirques, and verdant, U-shaped valleys. The best views can be found atop the tallest peak, Plomb du Cantal (6,085 feet/1,855 m), accessible via cable car and hiking trails.

But the park also offers picturesque villages with volcanic stone architecture, fat cows, vineyards, and rolling fields of sunflowers, adding a genteel and domesticated touch to this rugged land. Auvergne has its own celebrated local-based gastronomy. Salted

PICTURE
PERFECT

A climber plummets off the face off the mountain Ceuse, in southern France. Often described as one of the world's best climbing crags, this limestone pillar offers thrilling climbing routes, and a good incentive to rope yourself in (the pictured climber did). "This photo was taken at the end of a full day," says photographer Keith Ladzinski. "I held my position shooting colorful silhouettes, moving around to keep the necessary separation from climber to rock, when unexpectedly he took this big fall."

IMAGE BY KEITH LADZINSKI
National Geographic photographer

South Tirol
and the Dolomites

No place better epitomizes Europe's shifting borders and ancient weathered valleys than Italy's Trentino-Alto (South Tirol). The autonomous region of German-speaking Italy is dominated by nine mountain chains, including the bald, rocky-cropped Dolomites, and several meandering ranges of the Alps. This is the rarefied rooftop of Italy, with stupendous heights and lush valleys.

Though it borders both Austria and Switzerland in northern Italy, South Tirol is not to be confused with Tirol in Austria. Once all a part of the Austro-Hungarian Empire, this part of Tirol was annexed to Italy in 1919 after World War I. Remnants of the fierce fighting between the Austrians and Italians during that war still litter these wild mountains today. Trenches, sniper galleries blasted in the rock, and mountains whose peaks shattered in explosions—all this is evident on a hike through the Dolomites along the southern front line of fighting.

But World War I is merely yesterday when it comes to this region. It has a human history that stretches back to at least the third millennium B.C., when Ötzi the Iceman lived and roamed in these mountains. He was slain, an arrow to the back, and his body frozen in a glacier for millennia until he was famously discovered by hikers in the Ötztal Alps in 1991. The 5,300-year-old mummy was remarkably well preserved, and his DNA and remains yielded unexpected insights into the region's prehistoric peoples.

South Tirol has seen a parade of civilizations and cultures. It

In the shadow of the Dolomites, lop-eared sheep graze along the one-time front line of World War I (opposite).
The meadows bloom with flowers like Veronica chamaedrys (above).

was once a northern Roman settlement, and through the Middle Ages was home to the pillaging Ostrogoths, Franks, Bavarians, and Lombards in succession. They each left behind archaeological traces of their habitation in this wild landscape. (Ötzi himself and artifacts from other eras are on display in the South Tyrol Museum of Archaeology in the region's capital city, Bolzano.)

But South Tirol's serrated mountain profiles leave the deepest impression on today's visitors. This is the home to Italy's most scenic highland gems such as the lush, rolling green fields of Seiser Alm, the largest high-altitude Alpine meadow in Europe. The sheer,

REWIND A LONG WAY DOWN

The names of these adventurers and even the exact location of this climb have been lost to time, but sometime around 1913, two climbers made a harrowing pass between two sheer peaks in the Italian Dolomites or Alps. They used a technique called the "Tyrolean traverse," which involves merely setting a line between two high points to cross a gaping space between them. This photo originally accompanied a 1913 *National Geographic* magazine account of mountaineering in the Swiss Alps by Walter Woodburn Hyde, and chronicled in particular his ascent of Mont Blanc.

Though the caption accompanying this image is vague on the details of this particular climb, it does sagely note, "The rock-climber must possess a steady head, a sure foot, considerable gymnastic skill, and, above all, careful judgment . . . Some idea of the difficulties of rock work can be formed from this picture, where the least mistake in swinging between the two peaks means instant death." Indeed.

toothy Mount Schlern of the Dolomites juts into the sky above the meadow like a godly pedestal, and its stark peaks are noticeably different than the neighboring softer, greener Swiss Alps.

Among the most spectacular valleys in the Dolomites is the picturesque Val Gardena. By winter, it is blanketed in glistening white powder, with rocky, snow-dusted peaks etched against blue skies and deep green conifers laden with silvery snow. This is a wonderland for those who love winter sports: Val Gardena, one of 12 ski areas in the region, is considered the best skiing. But the region is no less enticing when the drifts melt away. Then it becomes a land of contrasts: Green slopes incline gently upward only to drop away into shadowy, vertical cliffs. Meadows are strewn with wildflowers and are bordered by dense stands of conifers—

Deep white powder and good company draw visitors to Berghaus Zallinger on the Seisser Alm, Europe's largest high-altitude meadow.

all surrounded by stony, precipitous mountain peaks that can support only snow bowls, even in the height of summer.

The valley is also one of only five in Italy where Ladin—an endangered dialect of the Dolomites—is still spoken. It can be heard at many of the *Buschenschänke* (rustic, traditional restaurants) and *Hofschänke* (mountain taverns) that dot the valley and serve up delicious Italian mountain fare. Try polenta topped with wildflowers, plates of *speck,* a mountain air-smoked ham, herb-flecked *knödel* (dumplings), and local wines like Gewürztraminer, Müller-Thurgau, Lagrein, and Blatterle.

TRAVELWISE

- **HOW TO VISIT** South Tirol is best accessed by car. The closest major airport hubs are Milan, Verona, and Innsbruck. Train connections emphasize north-south routes between Austria and Germany and southern Italy. Connections from western areas like Switzerland are possible, but limited and time-consuming.

- **PLANNING** The South Tirol website has info on UNESCO World Heritage sites to ski lifts and sought-after restaurants (*suedtirol.info/en).*

- **HOW TO STAY** Located at an altitude of 5,062 feet (1,543 m), the 55-room, horseshoe-shaped Alpenroyal Grand Hotel (*alpenroyal.com)* is perched on the Kurat swimming lake. It is located on the Via Ferrata walking trail, an ideal launching point for hikes and mountain bike tours.

PICTURE PERFECT

After photographing exotic locales around the globe, Italian photographer Ulla Lohmann realized she didn't know her own backyard. So she and her husband set out on a 155-mile (250 km) journey across the Dolomites. Even though they reached the 9,340-foot-high (2,847 m) Cima d'Asta in midsummer, the temperature was well below zero Celsius. "I didn't have gloves," she says. "But I didn't feel cold—until I realized that I couldn't move my fingers to press the shutter. It was one of those moments when I was only aware of the beauty of nature around me and the magic in the air."

IMAGE BY ULLA LOHMANN
National Geographic photographer

Rügen Island

In 1818, German artist Caspar David Friedrich visited the chalk cliffs of Rügen Island with his wife on their honeymoon. His oil painting of two figures overlooking the ivory cliffs out to the Baltic Sea remains to this day the most iconic image of the region. He was working with outstanding raw material, though: These breathtaking precipices are part of Jasmund National Park on the picturesque German island, a mile off the Pomeranian coast of the mainland.

The 357-square-mile (925 sq km) Rügen Island has been a favorite seaside destination since the 19th century, and the elegant resort architecture of that era attests to the island's early popularity. The cliffs, located along the island's Stubbenkammer promontory, are ancient. They were formed by a glacier that thrust the ocean floor upward to form a white coastal wall of chalk, clay, sand, and mudstone, which over the ages became embedded with fossils. The Baltic Sea dashes against pale rock at the foot of the cliffs, and a lush beech forest crowns their towering heights.

The best way to see the cliffs is along the cliff-top Hochuferweg trail that winds through the sun-dappled beech forests from the town of Sassnitz in the south to Lohme, farther north. An amble along this path offers great views of the cliffs and the flashing blue-green waters of the Baltic Sea. It is also a joy for nature lovers, who spot rare plants and magnificent birds, including white-tailed eagles, kingfishers, and peregrine falcons. The path passes some

The soft greens of the woodlands of Jasmund National Park on Rügen Island (opposite) contrast with the cheerful colors of pebbles on its beaches (above).

of the region's most distinctive features, including the best-known cliff of the coastline, Königsstuhl, or the "king's chair." This nearly 400-foot (122 m) precipice is perhaps best seen from the nearby Victoria viewpoint, which looks back at the luminous white cliff against a backdrop of sky and sea.

Though the essential elements of this shoreline are still intact, it looks different than it did in Caspar David Friedrich's day. The cliffs change each time storms or spring thaws send shells and rocks raining off them and onto the beaches below. Still, hikers along the Hochuferweg path are often hoping to find the same view that inspired the famous Friedrich painting (it now hangs in

a museum in Winterthur, Switzerland) 200 years ago. For many years, they were directed to the Wissower Klinken viewpoint, where two pointy chalk ridges framed a view out over the Baltic that strongly evoked the painting. Sadly, a 2005 landslide at this part of the cliffs carried away the spiny outcrops, though there is still a magnificent overlook across the water. (If it's a comfort, the scene in Friedrich's painting may not have been created from this vantage point anyway—most scholars agree that he was working from memory rather than life.)

Along the coastal path on the way to Königsstuhl, a path and steps lead down to the beach at the base of the cliffs. The view of

REWIND

In this photo from the early 1970s, taken outside the northern German town of Wismar, about 100 miles west of the Baltic Sea, women harvest sugar beets, trying to beat the frost. When *National Geographic* writer John J. Putman visited Germany to research a story for the magazine's September 1974 issue, East Germany was under Soviet control and farming was collectivized. East German women outnumbered men because of World War II casualties and because so many people had fled to West Germany in 1961 before the Berlin Wall sealed off the escape route. The population growth rate was near zero.

Putman got his story, but he faced challenges during his cold war–era travels in Soviet-controlled East Germany. "I found many East Germans still reluctant to talk with Western journalists," he wrote, "frequently described by their government as likely spies and provocateurs.

violent storm has stirred up the sea and washed debris ashore.

But precious as amber and fossils are, Rügen's most intriguing treasure has never been found—if it even exists. According to legend, the famous 14th-century German pirate Klaus Störtebeker buried a trove of gold on the island in a cave beneath the chalk cliffs that has never been discovered. (Lest this inspire you to treasure hunt, note that many spots along the park's 7-mile/11.2 km beachfront are inaccessible.)

TRAVELWISE

- **HOW TO VISIT** Jasmund National Park can be reached by car (about three hours from Berlin) or by train from Berlin or Hamburg. Königsstuhl is the most accessible of the cliffs, located just a few minutes from the interactive exhibits and visitor services of Königsstuhl National Park Center.

- **PLANNING** The website for the Königsstuhl National Park Center has great information for this region (*koenigsstuhl.com/en*).

- **HOW TO STAY** The island's classic seaside towns offer accommodations, but the most memorable options are perched on the cliffs, like Panorama Hotel Lohme (*panorama-hotel-lohme.de*; German).

Rügen Island's famous chalk cliffs face the sun as it rises over the blue expanse of the Baltic Sea.

the chalk cliffs from this sea-level perspective is very different, as you crane your neck trying to apprehend their sheer heights. The pebbly beach itself is worth combing for treasure. Some visitors search for chalk—the rocks that shear off the cliffs will indeed mark blackboards and sidewalks. Some look for fossils of ancient marine life. Others hunt for Baltic amber, fossilized resin that's 44 million years old. The best time to find this shimmering brown-orange stone, often used in jewelry, is after a

PICTURE PERFECT

Rügen Island's imposing chalk cliffs, with the 390-foot-high (119 m) Königsstuhl (King's Chair) towering above the Baltic Sea, are the centerpieces of Jasmund National Park. In this region, weather is famously moody, and as nature and wildlife photographer Norbert Rosing says, "It took a long time to get the right conditions [for this shot]." Those included safe flying weather, an available plane, and the right light. "In the afternoon, the coast is in shadow," says Rosing—so he had to wait for clear morning weather to capture the vibrant greens and blues of the beech trees and sky.

IMAGE BY NORBERT ROSING
National Geographic photographer

Engadine Valley

The special "diamond dust light" of the mighty Engadine Valley has been drawing visitors for over three centuries. These include the likes of the great German composer Richard Strauss and the famous writer Rainer Maria Rilke, all enticed by a dazzling atmospheric display created on cold winter days by innumerable, many-faceted ice crystals lingering in the atmosphere and glittering in the sun.

The Engadine Valley in Switzerland follows the Inn River, a tributary of the Danube, and stretches for 186 miles (300 km) in the eastern Swiss Alps. It runs from the Italian- and Swiss German–speaking village of Maloja near the Italian border to the wild, rugged, and remote Romansh-speaking village of Scuol on the Austrian border (Romansh is a dwindling regional language, akin to Latin), before plunging into Austria.

Within Switzerland, the Engadine is divided into two distinctly different segments: the ritzy Upper Engadine, home to St. Moritz, a high-end ski resort town, and the wild, unmanicured Lower Engadine, where ibex, chamois, and marmots run free in Switzerland's rugged 42,000-acre (17,000 ha) Swiss National Park.

The light of the valley is the most striking in winter, when ice dust trapped in the upper atmosphere catches the sun and casts an iridescent sparkle onto the snow-blanketed landscape. Come spring, it warms to a glow that spills over the pastel Alpine wildflowers, before softening in summer to a delicate, refined light. In autumn, the Engadine light flashes across the valley's copper foliage.

The bright red Glacier Express curves over the Landwasser Viaduct on the Rhaetian Railway (above).
Its route links Zermatt at the foot of the Matterhorn to beautiful St. Moritz (opposite) in the Upper Engadine Valley.

And of course, there are attractions beyond the light. The Upper Engadine is dotted with medieval castles, stylish resorts, and soothing thermal baths. But the small villages are perhaps even more charming—art lovers will appreciate the sgraffito seen on the Engadine's high-alpine Ofen (or Fuorn) Pass. The decorative pastel murals are a signature of the Graubünden region, and are painted carefully on the whitewashed houses. The road through the pass continues east to the peaceful Müstair Valley, and the Benedictine Convent of St. John at Müstair, an eighth-century abbey celebrated for its Carolingian-era frescoes and Romanesque apses.

Visitors who want a particularly scenic—and sometimes unnerving—approach to the Engadine Valley should catch a train from Zürich. Part of the three-hour trip travels along the Rhaetian Railway, which dives into jagged rock tunnels and threads its way across the towering Landwasser Viaduct that spans the Landwasser River at height of more than 200 feet (61 m).

The Swiss National Park within the rugged Lower Engadine (left) invites exploration in every season, with remote corners that can be reached by foot or on skis (above).

TRAVELWISE

• **HOW TO VISIT** Switzerland's airports and train stations are some of the world's best connection hubs. Zürich Airport, the country's largest, has dozens of direct international flights. From there, visitors can approach the Engadine Valley by car or train.

• **PLANNING** Switzerland Tourism's website has exhaustive information on almost every site in the country, plus travel logistics and accommodation guides (*myswitzerland.com*).

• **HOW TO STAY** The ski-in-ski-out Nira Alpina is 3 miles (5 km) from glitzy St. Moritz. Its 70 rooms feature soft down-topped beds, spruce paneling, and striking views of Lake Silvaplana (*niraalpina.com*). The more affordable Sporthotel Pontresina is 5 miles (8 km) from St. Moritz (*sporthotel.ch/en*).

Białowieża National Park

Białowieża Forest is the last remnant of an enormous primeval lowland forest that once stretched thousands of miles across the European Plain, from the Atlantic to the Ural Mountains. In this precivilization landscape, the giant European bison roamed freely. The magnificent beast barely escaped extinction in the 20th century, but Białowieża is now home to the continent's largest population.

Białowieża's old-growth forests, meadows, and riparian stands spill across two countries, Poland and Belarus, each of which has protected part of the territory as Białowieża National Park. In the 15th century, Polish royals declared Białowieża a private hunting reserve and actively managed the forest's landscape and the large game animals that roamed it. Nevertheless, the forest remained largely unadulterated until the early 20th century, when World War I tore across Europe and Białowieża, leaving in its wake poached animals and felled timber. In 1919, the last European bison living in the wild was killed here. Spurred to action, scientists in Poland began reviving the species, and in 1952 the bovine was once again released into the forest.

Bison numbers have since strengthened to over 500 free-roaming animals in the national park (900 in the entire forest) and several dozen more in captivity. The latter are kept primarily in the European Bison Show Reserve, where visitors have better odds of seeing them up close. In the wild, they are best spotted in the predawn hours, when they can be found grazing grasses and sedges or

The lush greenery of Białowieża National Park (opposite) offers a glimpse into Europe's great primeval lowland forest. The woods are populated by red fox (above).

browsing leaves and bark. Wolves, Eurasian elk, wild boar, lynx, martens, badgers, otters, and ermines number among the park's other robust mammal populations.

The forest has as much deadwood as it does living, and this is actually critical to the health and sustenance of many of its species. Trees that have been dead hundreds of years stand upright or fall to the forest floor and support thriving populations of birds, insects, lichen, and moss. Healthy populations of broad-leaved and evergreen trees such as lime, hornbeam, spruce, and alder also flourish in Białowieża.

Lumber has long been the building material of choice in this region of the world. Polish royals and Russian czars used it for their hunting lodges, relics of which are still scattered throughout the park. This timber architecture is on impressive display at the Palace Park, a compound of manicured gardens and wooden buildings that once serviced a 19th-century czarist hunting palace. The finest example, a timber-frame, ornately gabled manor house used by the governor of Grodno, dates to 1845 and is the oldest surviving building in the park. A wooden gate at the entrance to the Strict Reserve (the park's most protected inner sanctum) is all that remains of the czar's palace after a devastating fire in 1944. The Nature and Forest Museum now stands on this site.

Excursions into the Strict Reserve are led by park-licensed guides, and could include a break-of-dawn or dead-of-night jaunt into the heavy woods to spot bison and beaver. Bird-watching is a year-round activity, but the snowy backdrop in winter is ideal for glimpsing the red crest of a middle spotted woodpecker. It's a time when icicles drip from snow-dusted conifers, paw prints pepper the snow, and horse-drawn sleighs jingle through the woodlands of Białowieża.

TRAVELWISE

• **HOW TO VISIT** From Warsaw, rent a car or take the 4.5-hour daily bus to the village of Białowieża. For tickets and access to the Strict Reserve, hire a park-licensed tour operator like PTTK (english.pttk.pl) or Pygmy Owl Nature Tours (bialowiezaforest.eu).

• **PLANNING** Resources for planning are in Polish; you can translate the pages to English (bialowieza-forest.com; bpn.com.pl).

• **HOW TO STAY** Hotel Żubrówka (hotel-zubrowka.pl) has all the trappings of a luxury resort plus Nordic walking poles for snow treks. Guestrooms at the cozy Stoczek 1929 (en.www.stoczek1929.pl) are accented with hand-painted Polish ceramic sink bowls. The in-house restaurant serves Polish, Belarusian, Jewish, and Russian home cooking.

European bison, also known as wisents, differ from their American relatives in both skeletal structure and behavior.

Meals are offered within the former train station built for Tsar Nicholas II, who summered in the Białowieża Forest.

PICTURE PERFECT

Photographer Raymond Gehman captured this scene of a Polish child walking along a snowy road in the dead of winter in Białowieża Forest. At the time, Gehman was shooting in the northernmost location he'd ever worked. "It was very cold and the day-light hours were very short," he says. "Due to the isolated rural location, there were no snowplows for the roads. Villagers and farmers got around with horses and sleighs." Gehman took this shot when the boy in the photo asked to show him something in the woods, and walked ahead to lead the way.

IMAGE BY RAYMOND GEHMAN
National Geographic photographer

Plitvice Lakes National Park

Deep in central Croatia's dark, primordial Dinaric Alps, water and rock create the shimmering "land of the falling lakes," as Plitvice National Park is known. Gushing waterfalls plunge from 16 terraced, luminous, aqua blue lakes, coursing through wild beech and fir forests in a landscape that was known by 17th-century explorers as "Devil's Garden"—but Plitvice Lakes is far more like paradise.

The interconnected lakes—divided into the "upper lakes" and "lower lakes" sections—are separated by travertine dams over which water cascades as it descends roughly 425 feet (130 m) over some 5 miles (8 km). Established as a national park in 1949, then granted World Heritage status in 1979, Plitvice Lakes comprises 115 square miles (300 sq km) of water, forest, and mountains, making it Croatia's oldest and biggest park.

More than 1.1 million visitors flock each year to Plitvice to walk along a network of trails and wooden boardwalks around and over waterfalls, streams, caves, and interconnected lakes. The lower lakes are the most spectacular, boasting the nation's highest waterfall, 250-foot (76 m) Veliki Slap. Electric boats, buses, and trains make it easy to get around (swimming is prohibited). But with all this aboveground beauty to divert them, visitors miss the phenomenon taking place beneath the earth that makes the park truly significant.

It all begins with rainfall. Over millions of years, water has collected in the Dinaric mountains' basin of porous karst rock,

The blue-green lakes, falls, and woods of Plitvice National Park (opposite) are home to the European green lizard (above), which can be 16 inches (41 cm) long—two-thirds of that being its tail.

In Plitvice National Park, 16 interconnected lakes change color with the light.

In 1961, photo editor Gilbert M. Grosvenor—who would later go on to become president of the National Geographic Society—made his third visit to Yugoslavia in six years, navigating the new and often rustic coastal roads in what is present-day Croatia. World War II had devastated Yugoslavia—Grosvenor at one point observed that an entire generation of men between the ages of 35 and 50 was missing. Nonetheless, he tried to document the country's progress, and the industrial and economic strides that had been made since the war. He snapped this photo of gleeful children skipping steps in Dubrovnik's old quarter, on the Adriatic Sea.

Especially in the wake of a gutted generation, youth were precious to Yugoslavia. When Grosvenor asked one local official why the country seemed to be suffering an exodus of the young, the man reflected and then remarked glumly: "Young people are the same the world over. They expect fried chicken to fall from the sky."

seeping into a vast labyrinth of enormous caverns connected by winding passages. Here, over time, the water leaches calcium carbonate (lime) from the stone. Eventually the water pushes through the underground maze and, carrying the lime with it, makes deposits along the way, creating underground stalagmites and stalactites.

Finally, the subterranean torrent of water rushes out of the maze to the surface, where the lime crystals in the waters attach themselves to anything they come in contact with—mosses, blue-green algae, the mucus secreted by bacteria. Layers of lime form and eventually petrify, becoming travertine. The travertine in turn builds up over time into dams over which the waters continue to

flow and—voilà!—the exquisite scene before your eyes is born.

Given their porous nature, the travertine barriers are extremely fragile. Their survival was tested during the Croatian War of Independence (1991 to 1995), compounded with damage caused by fishing with dynamite and unregulated hunting. Wildlife and birds are really only just beginning to return to the landscape. There's a small population of European brown bears, which once were abundant throughout Europe. Voles, dormice, shrews, deer, wild cats, and an occasional wild boar seek refuge here as well. Even wolves are returning to this important refuge, as are Eurasian lynx—several pairs are believed to live here now, though you're unlikely to see the big cats.

And then there's the butterflies, clouds of multihued winged beauties flitting about the waterways and greenery, including the purple and lesser purple emperors with shocks of indigo decorating their delicate wings, and a selection of pale-shaded blues like the short-tailed blue and Chapman's blue butterflies.

Chub, rudd, and five kinds of trout swim in the pellucid waters of the lakes, and 157 bird species, including black storks, capercaillie, and pygmy owls, live here as well. In this unique setting, you'll also find some of Earth's rarest amphibians. Perhaps the oddest is the olm, a fully aquatic, blind salamander that inhabits subterranean caves in complete darkness. When they were first discovered in the 17th century, the pink, snakelike salamanders—which can live past 100—were mistaken for dragon larvae.

This enchanted landscape is evolving even now, with the gradual formation of new dams, new cascades, and new rivers. The seasons each bring their own aesthetic: Spring finds the waterfalls at peak capacity; autumn frames the cascades with a canopy of flaming foliage; and winter turns the falls to icicles.

Winter turns the falls at Plitvice into icicles, and the still waters of the lakes mirror the white, frosted landscape (opposite).

▶ TRAVELWISE

• **HOW TO VISIT** Zagreb International Airport is the closest airport. The park has two entrances: Entrance 1 accesses the lower lakes; and Entrance 2 accesses the upper lakes (closed in winter). You'll need a car to reach the park, though day tours are available from Zagreb and Split. Summer may find Plitvice crowded, and the falls reduced to a trickle.

• **PLANNING** The UNESCO site has info (whc.unesco.org/en/list/98); so does the Plitvice Lakes Tourist Board (tzplitvice.hr).

• **HOW TO STAY** There are three hotels next to the park (near Entrance 2); and Korana Camping Ground, about 4 miles (6 km) from the park, has bungalows and campsites. There are also plenty of accommodations in nearby towns and villages (including Slunj).

PICTURE
PERFECT

"Sometimes you have to remove yourself from the scene in order to capture it properly," says Jonathan Irish, whose assignment was to photograph the essence of Plitvice Lakes' watery landscape. "I knew if I could get an overhead view of the boardwalk it would be a special shot." He quickly hiked up a pathway to the top of the gorge and focused on a view that captured the boardwalk's S shape. But it wasn't a done deal quite yet. "In order to get a clear shot," he says, "I needed to . . . dangle over the edge while holding onto a tree for stability."

IMAGE BY JONATHAN IRISH
National Geographic photographer

Albanian Alps

The Accursed Mountains—perhaps it's that foreboding nickname that keeps development away from this pristine alpine pocket of northern Albania. That's a good thing. Little known and imposing, these ancient massifs of the Albanian Alps soar to heights of 8,835 feet (2,693 m) and harbor aquamarine waterfalls, ancient towpaths, and bridges carved into the golden-hued karstic rock.

The Albanian Alps, called the Malësia (highlands) in the local Albanian Gheg dialect, are part of the rugged, snowcapped Dinaric Alps that stretch across the western Balkan Peninsula. Unlike the Pyrenees and the Swiss Alps, which have been reshaped by modern agriculture and tourism, there is no shortage of wilderness here. Endemic wolves, lynx, and bears still roam the mountains, while endangered Alpine wildflowers and brilliantly mottled butterflies draw naturalists from all over the world.

From the west, the sapphire-hued Lake Komani is the typical gateway to Albania's Alps, and many guidebooks suggest it as an ideal entry portal. But sadly, the glacial lake is often strewn with plastic waste and in dire need of cleanup, a reminder of this region's status as an emerging world destination. Visitors are better off heading to picturesque Alpine farm villages like Quku i Valbonës where they can experience the deliberate, hardworking pace of the region's day-to-day life. Here you'll encounter the friendly *Malësori* (highlanders), a threatened mountain community that carries on traditions they've practiced for centuries. The men work in the

Rugged and rocky, the steep valleys and imposing Albanian Alps (opposite) challenge hikers.
A wooden signpost (above) indicates this once forgotten country's spot on the Balkan backpacker trail.

fields, while the women, heads bundled in scarves, sweep their homes with brooms fashioned from branches.

From Quku i Valbonës, visitors can embark on several hikes. One traveler's favorite winds down the mountain along the southern banks of the Valbona River toward the bustling town of Bajram Curri. En route, hikers will encounter wild strawberries, abandoned farmsteads, fire salamanders, and thickly wooded old-growth beech forest.

Hiking aside, visitors should know that getting around in Albania—especially the more rural parts—is its own adventure. Car rentals are possible, but driving here can be unnerving. Car ownership was forbidden until 1991 when the country shed its communist regime, and drivers are still somewhat unpredictable, and good connecting roads, a luxury. The country's *furgons* may be the best way to get around. These small, air-conditioned buses leave only when they fill up with passengers, but take travelers anywhere in Albania for about $5 to $10.

Local families offer lodging in picturesque guesthouses like this one in Theth (above). It's a welcome respite for hikers like these (opposite), covering ground between Theth and the village of Valbona.

TRAVELWISE

- **HOW TO VISIT** The capital Tirana's Nënë Tereza Airport is the country's only international airport. It's best to approach travel in Albania with a loose schedule and a roll-with-it attitude. The country has a limited train network, and furgons are inexpensive, but operate on no fixed schedule.

- **PLANNING** Visit Albania's website includes an interactive map of the different regions (*Albania.al*); the site run by the proprietors of the following inns is also useful for planning (*journeytovalbona.com*).

- **HOW TO STAY** Bunk at cozy 5-room Rilindja or an 11-room Rezidenca (see directions on the website), both run by a former Brooklyn bookshop owner and her Malësori partner. They serve up hearty, local fare like tender wood-grilled lamb, and a house specialty, *patlixhan ne tave*, a zesty ratatouille with garlic and fresh parsley (*journeytovalbona.com*).

Quiver trees (kokerboom) in
Namaqualand, South Africa

Africa

Africa has a wealth of places ancient and untamed, from the storied Nile Valley and sandy, shipwrecked coastlines to a stone forest of knife-edged rock spires.

Nile Valley

Below the Nile River's cataracts near the city of Aswan, the Nile Valley undergoes what the ancients considered a miraculous transformation. For much of its journey across northern Africa, it passes through desert, but the 130 miles (210 km) of river between Aswan and Luxor are the most striking of the Nile's entire length; a fertile oasis that has nurtured Egyptian civilization for more than 5,000 years.

"It is the beginning of the softness and lushness of Egypt and the end of the wilderness Nile," wrote Alan Moorehead of Aswan in the early 1960s. And the city remains that way today. Palm-mottled islands float in the middle of the Nile and great dunes rise on the western bank, the start of a Sahara that sprawls all the way across Africa to the Atlantic. Tourists lounge on the terrace of the Old Cataract Hotel as did Agatha Christie, Winston Churchill, and other luminaries who have stayed there since it opened in 1899.

Whether one travels via modern riverboat or roughs it by sleeping on the deck of a chartered felucca, the journey between Aswan and Luxor offers a glimpse of an Egypt that has remained unchanged for centuries: the hustle and bustle of waterfront villages, the *fellaheen* (peasants) tilling and harvesting their fields, lateen-sailed feluccas flitting back and forth, and every so often, a monumental reminder that pharaohs once ruled over this stretch of river.

The temples around Aswan and farther down the valley expose the indelible relationship between the Egyptian people and their river. The ancients believed that the everlasting tears of the goddess

In the Karnak Temple complex at Luxor—built and expanded by successive pharaohs over two millennia—massive columns are carved with hieroglyphics (opposite). Sails tilted, a traditional boat called a felucca (above) makes its way along the Nile at sunset.

Isis—spawned by the death of husband Osiris—created and sustained the River Nile. Worship of her endured until the sixth century A.D. at the half-sunken Philae Temple. Downstream from Aswan, Kom Ombo Temple was dedicated to Sobek, the crocodile god who was believed to have magical powers that kept Egypt safe from waterborne catastrophe. The Temple of Edfu was the site of a great riverside festival in olden days while the town of Esna, venue for another great pharaonic shrine, was called Latopolis in ancient times in deference to the Nile perch *(Lates niloticus)*.

Armant Island offers a last splash of arcadian countryside before the river drifts into Luxor. The massive Temple of Luxor rises on the right bank, the Temple of Hatshepsut is chiseled into ocher cliffs in the west, and beyond that looms the Valley of the Kings. A great way to conclude a journey down the Nile is to linger along the Corniche at dusk, watching the sun sink over the river and imagining that the pharaohs would have cherished the same view.

The lighted suburbs of Luxor (left) snake their way along the Nile toward the Valley of the Kings. A statue of the Egyptian pharaoh Ramses II guards Luxor Temple (above).

▶ TRAVELWISE

• **HOW TO VISIT** Fly south from Cairo to either Luxor or Aswan and board a multiday cruise along the Nile. With triple-digit temperatures nearly every day in summer, winter is the best time to visit Upper Egypt.

• **PLANNING** Egypt Tourism Authority has info on Luxor and Aswan *(egypt.travel)*; Abercrombie & Kent Egypt arrange Nile cruises *(akegypt .com)*; and Nile Dahabiya does riverboat charters *(nile-dahabiya.com)*.

• **HOW TO STAY** While on land, crash at historic properties like the Old Cataract Hotel in Aswan or the Winter Palace in Luxor (both hotels, *sofitel.com*; enter city names into the search bar). On the water, choose between passage on a modern riverboat, charter an opulent private boat, or hire a humble felucca and sleep on deck beneath the stars.

Lake Tana and Blue Nile Falls

The civilizations of ancient Egypt needed the mighty Nile River to flourish. And for that life-giving course of water, the pharaohs had Lake Tana partially to thank—it forms the headwaters of one of the Nile's two major tributaries. Floating at nearly 6,000 feet (1,829 m) above sea level, the lake is roughly the size of Tokyo, vast and tranquil. Sprinkling its shores and islands are ancient, secluded monasteries.

Lake Tana's copper-colored water is calm, quietly lapping against the lonely islets and peninsulas that dot its expanses. Save for the traditional fishermen casting nets, and paddlers transporting firewood on papyrus canoes, the vast basin appears peaceful and silent. This calm tableau is a fitting backdrop for the ascetics who keep Ethiopia's Christian heritage alive in the centuries-old monasteries built on the islands around the lake. These religious sanctuaries are unique from any other edifices in Christendom. The exquisite murals decorating their walls are based on the tradition of Byzantine and Italian icons, but have a distinctive use of color and form. Though most of the monasteries are religious sites closed to visitors, you can see exceptional monuments like Ura Kidane Mehret, a 16th-century Orthodox church whose round ambulatory is covered with vivid paintings depicting biblical scenes.

Lake Tana's tranquility contrasts drastically with the Blue Nile Falls that interrupt the sinewy Blue Nile just 18 miles (29 km) southeast of the lake's outlet. The water makes a thunderous commotion as it plunges nearly 150 feet (46 m). Many Ethiopians

The thundering Blue Nile Falls (opposite) interrupt the serene course of the Blue Nile from its headwaters in Lake Tana. On one of the lake's peninsulas, the 16th-century Orthodox monastery Ura Kidane Mehret is known for its murals (above).

believe the Blue Nile is the biblical river of Gihon, which is described in Genesis as flowing out of Eden. The landscape of acacia trees, euphorbias, and lush grasses do indeed make the setting of the falls seem a mystical garden. Scottish explorer and writer James Bruce described them in 1790 as being "half an English mile in breadth, with a force and noise that was truly terrible." Sadly, recent hydropower projects have stolen some of the falls' volume and power. In spite of this, they are still spectacular during the wet season from July to September, and the rising mist from their base explains their Amharic name, Tis Abay, meaning "smoke of the Nile."

From Blue Nile Falls, the Blue Nile travels through the impenetrable gorges of the Ethiopian Highlands before joining the White Nile in Khartoum, Sudan, to form the great Nile itself. The river then makes a vast journey, nourishing the river plains of Sudan and Egypt before eventually emptying out into the Mediterranean near the ancient Egyptian seaport of Alexandria.

People fish off a boat on the placid waters of Lake Tana (left). Bundles of freshly cut papyrus are off-loaded onto the shore of the lake (above).

TRAVELWISE

• **HOW TO VISIT** Use Bahir Dar, the lakeside city of 222,000 connected to Addis Ababa by frequent flights, as your home base, where you can look for private or group tours of the area. September and October yield impressive views of the falls, and temperatures are crisp.

• **PLANNING** First-time visitors may want to consider arranging a tour of northern Ethiopia's historic sites through operators like Cox and Kings, which plans itineraries (*coxandkingsusa.com*).

• **HOW TO STAY** Kuriftu Resort and Spa's lakefront stone bungalows have romantic four-post beds and terrace dining (*kurifturesortspa.com*).

Tsingy de Bemaraha

The world's fourth largest island, Madagascar, is sometimes touted as the eighth continent because its landscape and ecosystem are so distinctive. But a single glimpse of the spiny limestone needles of the stone forest in Tsingy de Bemaraha National Park and Reserve, and you might swear this corner of the Indian Ocean belongs to a different planet altogether.

Wind, water, and time have carved the karst topography of western Madagascar into a spectacular landscape of fluted limestone columns and rocky formations called *tsingy*. Owing to its inhospitable terrain, this stony jungle has kept out hunters, cattle ranchers, and even fire, enabling an unusual bionetwork of plants and animals to establish. If Madagascar—by nature of its island isolation—is a sanctuary from environmental hazards, the 586-square-mile (151,773-ha) Tsingy de Bemaraha Strict Nature Reserve and National Park is a haven within this haven.

As inhospitable as its landscape may seem, Madagascar harbors a staggering 5 percent of the world's wildlife species, and more than 80 percent of the species found on the island exist only here. Since it broke away from the African coast some 160 million years ago, Madagascar has forged its own path of evolution, engendering such animals as the hedgehog-like tenrec, the carnivorous, catlike fossa, and brilliantly plumed birds like the blue vanga.

Perhaps the tsingys' most mesmerizing residents are lemurs, primates that are native only to Madagascar and the neighboring

Suspension bridges, ladders, and steep paths bring humans into the spiny, unforgiving landscape of Madagascar's stone forest (opposite). An alert Madagascar kestrel (above) keeps watch over the landscape.

The massive, jagged rocks of the tsingy seem to defy the laws of gravity.

Comoro Islands. Said to resemble the earliest ancestors of primates, which existed tens of millions of years ago, these animals are found nowhere else on Earth, and can range in size from 20 pounds (9 kg) to a mere ounce (28 g). With their nimble claws to aid them, 11 species of lemurs navigate this serrated limestone maze. It may not provide leafy shelter, but lemurs hopscotch from one knife-edged pinnacle to another, leaping through the stone forest as effortlessly as antelope bounding through a field. It's not uncommon for visitors to spot families of these agile, wide-eyed creatures vaulting en masse from one peak to another.

The stone forest may have defied attempts at human settlement, but that doesn't mean humans haven't maneuvered their way in anyway. An excellent, modern network of mountain routes fixed with cables, ladders, boardwalks, and suspension bridges bring

REWIND A BOULDER-SIZE EGG

Perhaps even stranger than Madagascar's living animals are the creatures now extinct. One of these, the *Aepyornis maximus,* was a 10-foot-tall (3 m), half-ton flightless bird. *National Geographic* editor Luis Marden visited Madagascar in the 1960s in search of its massive, fossilized eggs. To his delight, the Geographic team came away with this giant specimen (pictured).

It was x-rayed back in Washington, D.C., and found to contain the embryo and skeleton of an aepyornis chick. One of the native Madagascans who had helped Marden search for the eggs had speculated, "The great bird was so tall that a man could not reach his head; he stood on long legs and had three toes on each foot, but no great toe, and no heel. His tail was spread out like a turkey's . . . His wings were very short, and when he ran, he did not flap his wings." Scientific reconstruction of the bird, Marden noted, suggested that this was an astonishingly accurate description.

visitors across the crevasses between spires. Hikers combat acrophobia as they cross the high bridges suspended between peaks, or twist and claw their way through narrowly situated rocks, and use every limb to navigate the terrain. Some of the caves that connect the trails can be too narrow for some tourists.

The travelers who brave these challenges and ascend the tsingy are rewarded with views of the rolling hills and savanna surrounding the stone forest. And the 360-degree panorama of the towering limestone spires alone is worth the climb. It's a vista reminiscent of a high-rise cityscape, but distinctly more organic—and menacing. The edges of the stone forest's "trees" are often sharp as a blade, and hundreds of feet tall.

To get a window into this austere landscape, visitors start with

A lemur called the Decken's sifaka is right at home among the razor-sharp spires of the stone forest.

the Petits Tsingy, where several circuits as short as an hour-and-a-half traverse relatively easy trail and bridges. You can also navigate through the gorges on traditional *lakana* canoes, gliding on tranquil water and into stalagmite grottoes. The truly impressive part of the park called Grands Tsingy is far less accessible. Though no climbing knowledge is required, a guided hike will reduce you to all fours at times. You may discover a new species of animal while you're exploring. Previously unknown miniature lemurs and frogs are just a couple of the species that have been discovered in recent years.

TRAVELWISE

• **HOW TO VISIT** The Tsingy de Bemaraha National Park is inaccessible during the rainy season from November through April. Even during dry months, the roads make it necessary to rent a 4WD. Individual travelers must hire a guide through the Madagascar National Park Office.

• **PLANNING** Book your guide before arriving (*parcs-madagascar.com*). Tour operators can take care of all logistics. National Geographic Expeditions offers 12-day Madagascar trips that include the Tsingy de Bemaraha National Park (*nationalgeographicexpeditions.com*).

• **HOW TO STAY** Hotels, bungalows, and campsites in the village of Bekopaka provide home base for travelers. Le Soleil des Tsingy Lodge has luxury cottages and an infinity pool (*soleildestsingy.com*).

PICTURE
PERFECT

"Many people have photographed this famous site," says photographer Cristina Mittermeier, who was on an assignment at western Madagascar's Avenue of the Baobabs when she captured this image. "I was lucky to be there after a rainstorm and when the light was so beautiful. Sometimes, staying a little later can bring the opportunity of finding magical light." The baobabs—sometimes called "upside-down trees" for their topsy-turvy stature—have been classified as an endangered species since 1998 due to an increase in rice field irrigation in the area.

IMAGE BY CRISTINA MITTERMEIER
National Geographic photographer

Samburu District

North of Mount Kenya, the terrain of Kenya evolves from forested highlands into a rust-colored wilderness that stretches more than 150 miles (241 km) across the northern part of the country before bleeding into the Turkana Desert. This is the traditional homeland of the Samburu people, who still decorate their hair and faces with an ocher clay that matches their earthy surroundings.

During the British colonial era, this region was called the Northern Frontier District and was basically the end of the Earth for those living in Kenya at the time. And it still has that far, faraway feel. It is a landscape that is at once handsome and ominous, and that blends romance, adventure, and even danger for those who stray too far into the bush. Much of the rest of Kenya may have been absorbed by farm and field, but not the wild and woolly Samburu District.

Much of the region now falls within the confines of national parks or wildlife conservancies. The latter are private or community lands where wild animals and humans coexist more or less in harmony, and benefit from the mutual relationship. The Samburu region's two dozen conservancies protect far more land than the government ever could and provide open range for pastoralists to graze their stock. It's not unusual, for instance, to see locals herding their cattle within eyeshot of rhino, buffalo, or even lions.

Nanyuki, a busy town on the northwest flank of Mount Kenya, is the gateway to the north both figuratively and literally—the Equator passes right through the town. On the outskirts of town,

Acacia trees are silhouetted at sunset in Meru National Park in central Kenya (opposite).
A curious reticulated giraffe peers over thornbush at Ol Pejeta Conservancy (above).

Ol Pejeta Conservancy is the southernmost end of a network of reserves that stretches all the way to Marsabit National Park in the far north. The conservancy's claim to fame is twofold: a large rhino population, and a chimpanzee sanctuary that harbors primates rescued around Africa.

Farther north is "Born Free" country, where George and Joy Adamson lived with their celebrated lioness, Elsa. Orphaned by hunters shortly after her 1956 birth, the cub was raised in Samburu National Reserve and spent her latter years with the Adamsons in Meru National Park. Her grave in Meru is a place of pilgrimage for those who have read or seen *Born Free*.

Anchoring the far north of the Samburu region is massive Marsabit National Park, set around a heavily wooded mountain and three volcanic crater lakes. You can actually get out of the Land Rover and stretch your legs at Marsabit, with a trek up the 5,600-foot-high (1,707 m) shield volcano that gives the park its name.

Colorful textiles enliven a village market in the small town of Wamba (left), part of Samburu County. A baby African elephant (above) stays close to its mother in Ol Pejeta Conservancy.

TRAVELWISE

• **HOW TO VISIT** Kenya's A2 highway runs from Nairobi to Marsabit through the heart of the Samburu region. Safarilink airlines serves Nanyuki, Lewa, Samburu Reserve, and Loisaba from Nairobi (*flysafarilink.com*).

• **PLANNING** Kenya Tourism Board offers general travel info for Kenya (*magicalkenya.com*); for more specific regional information, try the Northern Rangelands Trust (*nrt-kenya.org*).

• **HOW TO STAY** Most of the region's national parks and wildlife conservancies have lodges or tented safari camps. Good ones include Lewa Wilderness lodge (*lewawilderness.com*), Elsa's Kopje in Meru National Park (*elsaskopje.com*), and Loisaba Conservancy (*loisaba.com*).

NAMIBIA

Etosha National Park

The name Etosha means "great white place" in the language of the Ovambo people who have lived in this region since prehistoric times, and that's exactly what you'll find: a national park around Namibia's largest dry lake. The great Etosha Pan sprawls across more than 2,368 square miles (6,133 sq km) of scorched earth. Yet even during the driest times, Etosha attracts an incredible array of wildlife.

Formed roughly 100,000 million years ago, the lake was fed by a constant source of freshwater until around 14,000 B.C. when tectonic forces shifted the Kunene River to a more northerly course. Slowly but surely, the lake dried into a hard-baked pan so large that it's easily seen from space and so alien that it was used as a backdrop for parts of the film *2001: A Space Odyssey*. The pan throws up an almost constant mirage, a ghostly vision created by intense heat rising from the surface. Large animals sometimes wander onto the pan in search of salt licks or the saline-resistant grass that sprouts from the bed. But their movements are tightly restricted by the lack of drinking water.

The pan really springs to life during the rainy season between November and April when water flows into the Etosha expanse via the Ekuma, Oshigambo, and Omuramba Ovambo Rivers. Brackish ponds are formed, and bird life multiplies rapidly to take advantage of both the water and the isolated protection from predators. The most conspicuous arrivals are bright-pink flamingos, as many as a million of them wading through the shallow

Visitors watch the sun set from the viewing platform at Etosha Safari Lodge.

water and kicking up microscopic organisms they sift through their curved bills. They also construct small clay mounds in which they lay their eggs and rear the young.

During the rest of the year, artesian springs and man-made wells provide drinking water for Etosha's thirsty critters, water holes where a great variety of grazing animals and predators gather, especially near sunrise and sundown. Elephants often arrive in family groups of half a dozen or more, making hardly a sound as they approach the ponds. At any given time other creatures might arrive waterside—zebra, antelope, giraffe, and gemsbok, Namibia's national animal. Perhaps a pack of hyena on the hunt for scraps. Or maybe even a few of the black rhino or many lions that make Etosha home.

The pan spreads across about a quarter of Etosha National Park. The remainder of the vast reserve comprises mopane woodland and the occasional thorn bush savanna with acacia trees or open grasslands. When not poised around the water holes, the majority of Etosha's terrestrial species find food and refuge in the thick mopane. In addition to the more common species, Etosha provides a habitat for a number of seldom seen animals like the ground pangolin, aardwolf, serval cat, bat-eared fox, and brown hyena.

Namutoni Fort has been the gateway to Etosha since it reopened its gates in 1957, although the whitewashed bastion is actually much older. It is a relic of German colonial days that was rebuilt in 1906 after rampaging Ovambo tribesmen destroyed the first fort. In days gone by, the fort provided the park's only overnight

Zebras are among Etosha National Park's vast array of wildlife, which also includes flamingos, gemsbok, lion, and the elusive black rhino.

National Geographic journalist Douglas H. Chadwick went to Etosha National Park in 1983 to research a story on wildlife. This image captures park veterinarian Dr. Ian Hofmeyr, his assistant, and nature conservator Mike Heywood weighing a tranquilized—and hefty—wildebeest. The team was conducting a study on the populations of the animal in the park, which were in decline because of anthrax, restricted migration, and an increase in Etosha's lion population.

The latter was such a concern that at the time of Chadwick's visit, park biologists were experimenting with capturing the lions, giving them time-release contraceptives, and releasing them back to the wild. This had to be handled with care—Etosha's lions were huge. Chadwick said of one pride of big cats, "Here, then, were a dozen excellent reasons the park requires visitors to stay in their cars, particularly since the Okondeka pride is descended from a gang that ate several people years ago." The wildebeests, alas, had no cars to hide in.

probably the park's best chance of spotting the solitary and always elusive leopard. Onkoshi was opened in 2008, and is the only camp that's actually built on the lakeshore. And the launch of Dolomite and Olifantsrus Camps has enabled a limited number of visitors to explore the vast western end of the national park.

TRAVELWISE

• **HOW TO VISIT** Although visitors can sign up for fully guided trips, Etosha National Park is ideal for self-drive safaris. Rental vehicles are available in Windhoek, 300 road miles (483 km) south of Namutoni. The park is open year-round. The dry season (May to October) is best for game viewing at water holes, but winter (November to April) brings lush landscape, water on the pan, and birdlife.

• **PLANNING** Etosha National Park has an official website (*etoshanational park.org*); the Namibia Tourism Board has more information on traveling in the country (*namibiatourism.com.na*).

• **HOW TO STAY** Six tourist camps sit along the southern and eastern edges of the pan, and the park's western sector. They offer overnight accommodation in bungalows, permanent luxury tents, and campgrounds. Just outside the park, accommodations like Etosha Safari Lodge are set in mopane bush and woodland (*gondwana-collection.com*).

accommodation, and the gate was shuttered at night to keep out the wildlife. Nowadays it's a day use area with a restaurant and vintage towers that afford one of the few elevated views of the pancake-flat Etosha landscape.

Three other tourists camps are scattered around the southern and eastern shore of the pan. Okaukuejo, perched at the opposite end of the pan from Namutoni, was created in 1901 as a frontier outpost for the German colonial troops. About halfway along the pan's southern shore, Halali tourist camp is set amid natural *koppies* (rock outcrops) and surrounded by mopane forest. It provides

PICTURE
PERFECT

"This was taken at the end of a long day, when everything was settled down and peaceful," says Annie Griffiths of this image of a camper resting in the twilight at Sossusvlei, along Namibia's coastline. This barren, otherworldly landscape is about 500 miles (805 km) southwest of Etosha and is dominated by some of the world's tallest sand dunes—windswept, water-eroded massifs dating back 60 million to 80 million years.

IMAGE BY ANNIE GRIFFITHS
National Geographic photographer

Skeleton Coast

One of the planet's starkest, most unspoiled shorelines, the Skeleton Coast stretches more than 300 miles (483 km) along Namibia's northern seaboard between Walvis Bay and the Angolan border. Considered a deadly wasteland in years gone by, the coast is now cherished for its rich wildlife, a blend of sea creatures, desert critters, and savanna animals.

The coast boasts a long and notorious reputation. The indigenous Bushmen people called it the "land God made in anger." Portuguese mariners—sailing past the barren coast as they pioneered the route around southern Africa to India—dubbed it the Areias do Inferno (meaning "sands of hell"). And 19th-century Swedish explorer Charles John Andersson quipped that "Death would be preferable to banishment to such a country."

The shoreline is strewn with remains of more than a hundred shipwrecks. Among them are the largely sand-shrouded *Eduard Bohlen* (ran aground 1909), the steamer *Otavi* (1945), the fish factory *Suiderkus* (1977), and the *Dunedin Star* (1942), subject of the tome by John Henry Marsh that gave the Skeleton Coast its name.

The coast's unique geography derives from a collision of two great natural forces—the cold Benguela Current flowing up from the polar waters of the South Atlantic and the winds of the Kalahari Desert blowing in from the east. Together they spawn a superdry onshore environment (where rainfall averages less than an inch a

Both sea and sand are rippled at the Skeleton Coast in Namibia, where the Atlantic Ocean meets the baking Namib Desert (opposite). Despite its name, the coast is home to lively creatures, including some 700,000 Cape fur seals (above).

year) and a rich offshore habitat where marine animals feast on the microscopic fodder produced by upwelling.

Although much of the shoreline is sandy, including prominent dunes, other landforms contribute to an intriguing geological mosaic of gravel plains, clay formations, lava fields, salt pans, and rocky beaches. Away from the shore, the landscape is dominated by desert mountains and valleys carved during the last ice age and eroded by intermittent streams and the few year-round rivers that flow from the Namibian interior.

Despite the harsh environment, wildlife on the Skeleton Coast is rich and varied. Dolphins, orcas, and humpback whales cruise the offshore waters. Hundreds of thousands of fur seals gather at Cape Fria and Cape Cross. Jackals and hyenas also patrol the shore, as does the occasional lion on the prowl for washed-up sea creatures. There's enough vegetation in the coastal valleys to support smaller subspecies of elephant and black rhino, as well as zebra, ostrich, gemsbok, springbok, giraffe, and baboons.

The coast was once inhabited by humans too, the so-called Strandlopers who hunted and gathered along this shore long before the arrival of the first Europeans in the 15th century. The seminomadic

Tire tracks crisscross the vast, lonely expanses of sand and dunes in the Namib Desert.

REWIND

This photo was taken in the early 1950s by Quentin Keynes, great-grandson of Charles Darwin and contributor to *National Geographic*. He took this shot on an expedition to Cape Cross, a headland off Namibia's Skeleton Coast. It shows the German reproduction of a stone *padrão* (pillar) that Portuguese explorer Diogo Cão had planted in the 15th century to mark his southernmost landing on the African coast. Cão himself disappeared into the mists of history after erecting this monument; whether he died at Cape Cross, or somewhere along the Congo River, or back in Portugal, has never been determined.

Centuries later, the Germans took possession of this land, and in the 1890s replaced the original cross with this reproduction (the original is in a museum in Berlin). This photo by Keynes was pulled from the National Geographic archives and accompanied a manuscript he wrote about southwest Africa, but it was never published, and until now this image has never seen print.

1970s. The creation of Dorob National Park in 2010 extended protection to the remaining stretch of wild coast between the Ugab River and south past Walvis Bay.

The Namibia government's hands-off approach to managing Skeleton Coast Park means there are no fences, few roads, and barely any visitor amenities. Primitive facilities are available at Terrace Bay and Torra Bay, but that's about it.

TRAVELWISE

• **HOW TO VISIT** Starting out from Swakopmund, visitors can drive Namibia Highway C34 along the entire length of Dorob National Park and across the southern half of Skeleton Coast Park as far as Mowe Bay. Fly-in specialists like Windhoek-based African Profile Safaris provide access to the park's remote northern shore (*www.profilenamibia.com*).

• **PLANNING** Namibia Tourism Board provides general info on travel in the country (*namibiatourism.com.na*).

• **WHERE TO GO** Along the shore are a lodge and campsite at Cape Cross (*capecrosslodge.com*), a campground at Torra Bay, and bungalows at Terrace Bay. There's better accommodation inland at places like Desert Rhino Camp in the Palmwag Concession (*wilderness-safaris.com*).

Himba people, who live just inland from the Skeleton Coast, continue the Strandloper tradition of largely living off the land.

For decades the coast was largely ignored, a place where wildlife could thrive in seclusion far away from harvesting and hunting, and where a landscape free of diamonds, gold, and other underground riches remained largely unscarred by human endeavor. Local authorities finally established Skeleton Coast Park in the

PICTURE
PERFECT

African penguins forage in the gin-clear waters of Namibia's Mercury Island, a rocky islet just off the Skeleton Coast's mainland. "Light is always an issue along this coast," says photographer Thomas Peschak. "In the morning, the island is often shrouded in thick fog, which only lifts later in the day when the light is harsher." Riptides and dangerous waves are an issue too. This image was taken at low tide, at a rare moment when massive swells were not present. "Getting pulled out to sea here is no joke," Peschak says. "The nearest opportunity for rescue is days away."

IMAGE BY THOMAS PESCHAK
National Geographic photographer

Namaqualand

In most seasons, the region known as Namaqualand looks like a sunbaked, sparsely populated wasteland. It stretches along South Africa's western coast for some 600 miles (966 km), across copper-veined hills, dusty mining towns, and sandy plains. But for a short period every year, after winter rains begin in late July or early August, this parched expanse explodes with wildflowers.

The dazzling number of blooms is what makes Namaqualand so enchanting—never-ending carpets of wildflowers in every color of the rainbow, transforming roadsides, fields, and enormous areas of scrubland into a stunning garden. Then again, it's not just about the numbers. It's also about the sheer variety of flowers that creates such an amazing sight. All in all, more than 3,500 species of flowering plants grow here, including the celebrated African daisy. About 1,000 of these flowers are found nowhere else on Earth.

The resilience of these desert plants is remarkable. Every plant must cope with low rainfall, and so remains inactive in the soil for possibly many years, germinating only when conditions are right. The methods these flowers use to adapt are ingenious: Succulents store water in their leaves or stems; trees grow deep roots to seek groundwater or stay near watercourses.

Plants must also compete to get their seed to germinate, and every single one has developed ways to attract the necessary bug pollinators. The petals of the beetle daisy, for example, are speckled with black, faux bug spots that lure bee flies looking to mate. And

Parts of Namaqualand are carpeted in bright wildflowers like the African daisy (opposite) after South Africa's rainy season. Small groups of zebra roam the hills (above) at places like the Goegap Nature Reserve.

goat's horn flowers (genus *Diascia*) release tiny but nutritious drops of oil; to get to them a bee has developed extra-long legs that are also ideal for spreading pollen.

So the question is, "Where's the best place to see the flowers?" Truth be told, a floral spectacle cannot be anticipated in any one place at any one time; it depends entirely on the amount of water and sun, and each year sees a different combination of those life-giving qualities. By the same token, the selection of flowers is different every year. The Namaqualand Flower Route, a five-hour drive north of Cape Town, loops through some of the most important flower sites in Namaqualand, and is one of the best bets for getting good views of the blooms.

Along the route, you'll find Richtersveld Cultural and Botanical Landscape, a World Heritage site northeast of Port Nolloth with over 300 types of plants found nowhere else in the world. Against a dramatic setting of deep canyons and saw-toothed mountains, the spectacular wildflower show here might include the rare kokerboom (or quiver tree), a tall branching aloe, as well as the strange, spiny, cactuslike halfmens tree, which always leans slightly to the north. Skilpad Wildflower Reserve, part of the bigger Namaqua National Park, is another reliable option, promising plenty of famed African daisies. And the Goegap Nature Reserve outside Springbok supports some 600 indigenous plant species and abundant animal life, including Hartmann's mountain zebra, aardwolf, honey badger, and antelope.

Wherever you go on your petal safari, be sure to get out and take a stroll among the flowers. Here, in this breathtaking land of brilliant blooms, you'll quickly understand the local saying: "You weep twice when visiting Namaqualand; first when you arrive, and then when you leave."

TRAVELWISE

• **HOW TO VISIT** The Namaqua region is a five hours' drive north of Cape Town along the West Coast Road; you'll need a car. Wildflower safaris are offered as well—inquire at local information offices. The wildflowers are in season late July to October. A series of drives that showcases the flowers centers on the towns of Garies, Springbok, Kamieskroon, and Port Nolloth.

• **PLANNING** Several websites have good resources for traveling in Namaqualand (*southafrica.net; experiencenortherncape.com; sanparks.org*).

• **HOW TO STAY** Springbok is the capital of Namaqualand and the best base—you'll find a good selection of hotels, bed-and-breakfasts, lodges, and guesthouses. The towns of Langebaan and Clanwilliam are good choices as well for their accommodations and proximity to wildflowers.

The best way to approach the flowers is from the north, as they face the sun.

These succulents, called "halfmen," have a semihuman appearance, complete with mops of crinkly leaves that resemble hair.

PICTURE
PERFECT

Gregarious and fun-loving, squirrel-size meerkats eke out a living in the drought-stricken South African plains. Their seemingly comical upright stance enables them to gaze alertly for danger far in the distance. "They are highly social and intelligent animals, and fun to work with," says photographer Mattias Klum. It took him several weeks to gain the trust of this group by approaching them very slowly. Meerkats learn to recognize danger and ignore animals that do not pose a threat—with patience and time, people fall into the latter group.

IMAGE BY MATTIAS KLUM
National Geographic photographer

Huangshan Mountain peeks above the clouds after a snowfall.

Asia

*Asia's remote marvels are both natural and human-made—
rock-cut cave sanctuaries, lakes carpeted with lotus blooms,
Buddhist monasteries, and enigmatic island hills.*

JORDAN

Coral Reefs of Aqaba

In Jordan, a country best known for its sand, dramatic *wadis* (ravines), and the rock-hewn metropolis of Petra, a small coastline has unexpected marine riches hidden beneath startlingly clear water. The breezy port city of Aqaba, only a dozen miles from the Saudi Arabian border, has a compact shore that may be one of the world's best diving and snorkeling spots.

Aqaba, sheltered from stormy weather at the head of a gulf off the Red Sea, has dodged the kind of overdevelopment that devastated the marine life off nearby resort towns like Sharm el Sheikh, Egypt. More than 5 miles (8 km) of Aqaba's southern coast has been preserved as a marine park, and as a result, the warm, crystal waters hold hundreds of different kinds of hard and soft corals. In addition to the mollusks, algae, amphipods, and starfish that populate the water, the shallow, dense reefs right off the coast provide home to a great number of fish that wend their way among the tubular sponges. Endangered hawksbill turtles gently wave through the water with black marbled flippers; the electric speckles of the blue-spotted ray warn predators of their toxic tails; and the canary-bright mouths of the yellow-mouthed moray eels are on display as they breathe. Shy clown fish dart in and out of the spaghetti-slim tentacles of sea anemone, and flamboyantly colored angelfish patrol the shallow water. The lionfish is considered an invasive pest in the Caribbean, the Atlantic, and as far afield as the Gulf of Mexico where it has no natural predators. But here it is merely a part

A red lionfish, its many fins waving, swims in the water above hard corals in the reefs off the city of Aqaba (opposite).
A colorful assortment of spices and foodstuffs are for sale in the Jordanian port city (above).

of the circle of life, and can be guiltlessly admired for its bizarre appearance, which includes a "mane" of striped fins and spines that drift along with the currents as it prowls the outer slopes of coral.

The lower waters of Aqaba maintain stable temperatures throughout the year, rewarding deep-sea divers with even more underwater spectacles and underwater visibility that can reach 100 feet (30.5 m). There are 21 dive sites that boast unique, watery attractions like the eerie hulk of the *Cedar Pride,* a cargo ship intentionally sunk to create an artificial reef in the 1980s and now covered with urchins, Spanish dancers, and crabs. In the Eel Garden, the snakelike fish winds its long, narrow body around sea grasses and coral pinnacles, and more fearsome, massive sea life like whale sharks and barracuda have been known to make an appearance among underwater canyons. On the other hand, divers may encounter such small, whimsical creatures as seahorses, many-colored nudibranchs, and perhaps even an octopus. A night dive may reveal shellfish like lobsters and crabs creeping about, too.

People have long been a presence along the gulf shores of Jordan, whether as tourists (left) or soldiers disputing borders, as evidenced by a M42 tank scuttled in 1999 to make an artificial reef (above).

▶ TRAVELWISE

• **HOW TO VISIT** Winter is the best time to visit Aqaba, when the sunshine is plentiful but not oppressive. Charter flights link Aqaba with many European gateways. Sinai Divers offers diving packages in Aqaba (*sinaidivers.com*); so does Aqaba Adventure Divers (*aqaba-diving.com*).

• **PLANNING** General information about the city and planning information is available at the Aqaba Tourist Information Center site (*aqaba.jo*). Aqaba Marine Park offers information on the park and on the coastal marine life (*aqabamarinepark.jo*).

• **HOW TO STAY** Your best bet is one of the diving specialist hotels that can guide you to prime diving spots, like Red Sea Dive Center, founded by a former Jordanian naval officer (*aqabascubadiving.com*).

Cave Monasteries of Davit Gareja

High in the cliffs of eastern Georgia's rugged and remote border with Azerbaijan is a complex of 19 medieval cave monasteries. Considered masterpieces of Georgian art, the earliest of these spectacular, rock-cut sacred spaces were established in the first half of the sixth century by one of the 13 Assyrian Fathers, St. David (Garejeli), and his disciples.

Patronized by kings and pilgrims, the caves at Gareja once housed nearly 5,000 monk cells, as well as barns, bakeries, and a school of fresco painting. The sacred caves were abandoned and used as a Soviet training ground during the 20th century, and today, only one of them—Lavra—is restored and functioning as a monastery. Monks still live there and, on occasion, can be heard chanting in the eerie silence of the deserted steppe. Visitors are welcome; however, appropriate dress—long pants for men, and a pashmina or scarf for women to cover the shoulders and head—is required.

From mid-April to the end of June, the slopes leading up to Lavra are typically blanketed with blooming wildflowers, colorful birds, and butterflies. You are more likely to get wet (and contend with slippery footing) in April and May, though, so visitors will want to pack rain gear and take it slow on the trail.

Udabno, another Gareja site well worth exploring, is a steep hike up from the Lavra monastery. This cave monastery is world renowned for its frescoes, which include an 11th-century mural of the Last Supper. The paintings in the Annunciation Church of

Cave monasteries (opposite) were carved into the soft sandstone of this part of Georgia starting in the sixth century.
Ancient murals can still be seen inside the Udabno monastery, including this one of the Last Supper (above).

this monastery date to the late 13th century, and feature dark, vivid colors and dramatic renderings of scenes like the raising of Lazarus, the Transfiguration, and Christ's entry into Jerusalem. Though they're well worth the effort, the paintings involve some vigorous cardio—specifically, you'll have to take at least a 60-minute (one-way) walk up a rocky path to reach them. When you stop to take a breath and admire the scenery at the crest of the Gareja mountain range, nod to the Azerbaijani border guard. Udabno, though culturally Georgian Orthodox, is located in predominantly Muslim Azerbaijan. Hikers visiting Udabno can freely pass over the border and back.

The frescoes are what draw visitors to Udabno, yet some of the best views here are from the inside out. Stand just inside any of the caves and peer out at the deserted and beautiful Azerbaijan steppe. The lunarlike landscape is a treeless sea of nothingness stretching as far as the eye can see.

The monastery of Lavra includes the 17th-century Georgian Orthodox Church of St. Nicholas (opposite). More than a dozen cave complexes are spread over the remote, windswept Kidron Valley (above).

TRAVELWISE

- **HOW TO VISIT** The Davit Gareja complex is a two-hour drive from Tbilisi. Wear hiking boots, and bring water and a trekking stick (for stability and to scare off the ubiquitous snakes).

- **PLANNING** Advantour offers day tours including round-trip transportation from Tbilisi hotels, a picnic lunch (no food or drinks are sold at the site), and an English-speaking guide (*advantour.com/georgia*).

- **HOW TO STAY** Owned by a British expat, the aptly named Hotel British House is an intimate alternative to Tbilisi's chain hotels. The historic inn (built in 1893) has nine rooms, one with a balcony. Rates include breakfast. Davit Gareja tours are available for an added fee (*british-house.ge*).

Band-e-Amir National Park

A chain of cobalt blue lakes flashes out of the craggy red-gray foothills of central Afghanistan's Hindu Kush mountains. This is Band-e-Amir National Park, a point of pride and a rare natural oasis in a country that has seen conflict for nearly 40 years. White travertine dams cup six clear lakes into natural infinity pools, and waterfalls cascade over the walls of the dams that separate them.

Band-e-Amir seems an anomaly, located as it is in the dry, mountainous terrain of Bamyan Province. According to one version of the Band-e-Amir creation story, Ali, cousin and son-in-law to the Prophet Muhammad, single-handedly brought this landscape into existence. An evil king, so the story goes, provoked Ali to harness the wild Band-e-Amir River. Ali swung his sword high above his head, lopped off part of the surrounding mountain, and stepped on top of it to stem the river's flow. The local villagers grumbled—the dam hindered their ability to irrigate the land. So Ali pressed his hand into the dam, leaving behind five falls where his fingers rested. The feat so impressed and terrified the king that he and his people converted to Islam on the spot.

With a little imagination, visitors to the national park can easily see those mythical fingerprints in the larger-than-life vistas in front of them. Giant flat-topped mesas and rocky peaks, soaring some 10,000 feet (3,050 m) above sea level, appear to part into a Grand Canyon–like gorge, making way for a connected series of elevated lakes, water cascading down mineral-formed dams like a staircase.

Set in Bamyan Province in the Hindu Kush mountains of central Afghanistan, Band-e-Amir National Park (opposite) encompasses six clear blue lakes that offer scenic respite and recreation to visitors (above).

There are only a few other instances of travertine lakes in the world, and, arguably, these six jewels have the most dramatic setting. Their names in Dari—Band-e Ghulāmān (Lake of the Slaves), Band-e Qambar (Lake of the Caliph Ali's Slave), Band-e Haybat (Lake of Awe), Band-e Panēr (Lake of Cheese), Band-e Pudina (Lake of Wild Mint), and Band-e Zūlfiqār (Lake of the Sword of Ali)—each highlight a different facet of the creation legend. A 20th-century shrine dedicated to Ali's handiwork is embedded into the cliff walls surrounding the Band-e Haybat, and pilgrims

REWIND AN ANCIENT PRAYER TOWER

Thomas J. Abercrombie, a member of *National Geographic*'s foreign editorial staff, explored some 20,000 miles (32,000 km) of Afghanistan by Land Rover, camel, horse, and yak around 1968. Nearly 250 miles (400 km) west of Band-e-Amir in Ghor Province, Abercrombie met Mohammed Azzam, an area elder and keeper of the Minaret of Jam, a 227-foot (70 m) brick tower built in the 12th century in the ancient kingdom of Ghor. Abercrombie and Azzam (pictured) climbed 20 stories on the tower's remarkable dual spiral staircases. Where Azzam stands, muezzins (or Muslim prayer callers) once stood to call the country to prayer—though by Abercrombie's visit, the region was largely deserted. It's not evident from this angle, but elaborate carvings and inscriptions cover the outside of the tower, and it leans at an angle of over three degrees.

The Minaret of Jam still stands today, but its existence is threatened by flooding from a nearby river and difficulties of restoration work in a remote area plagued by security issues.

come from miles to bathe in the icy-cold crystalline waters, said to have healing properties.

In geological reality, carbon dioxide-rich spring water eroded the limestone base rock to form the pools. The high concentration of carbon dioxide in the water contributes both to the electric ultramarine color of the lakes and to the calcium carbonate deposits that enclose them. Eons of deposits collected into the dams that wall the water bodies as high as 10 feet (3 m) above each other, creating distinctly different characters in each pool, where schools of fish and billowing aquatic plants live.

The area is a far cry from what it was just 10 years ago: Land mines plagued the land surrounding access roads, the lakes were littered with trash from a nearby bazaar, and cars parked on the delicate travertine surfaces. It wasn't until 2009 that Band-e-Amir

The waters in Band-e-Amir's lakes are high in carbon dioxide, which contributes to their startling teal color.

National Park was established—the first such designated space in Afghanistan. The park has consistently had some 130,000 annual visitors since, filling the many walking trails along the lakes and atop the northerly canyon rim that looks over them. New boardwalks and paved walkways that wind around the delicate geological dam structures are in the planning phases.

Populations of urial and ibex—large-horned ungulates—have been seen migrating through Band-e-Amir, and tiny jerboa (they look like a miniature cross between a rabbit and kangaroo) hop between rocks as eagles soar overhead. It is an area characterized alternately by quiet and howls of the whipping wind.

▶ TRAVELWISE

• **HOW TO VISIT** This destination demands equal parts adventure and caution. Roads connect Kabul to Band-e-Amir, a four-hour mountainous one-way drive; conditions are best April through October. Many of the park's 130,000 annual visitors are Afghan citizens. The few international travelers often opt to access the park via Bāmyān (about an hour east).

• **PLANNING** Little regularly updated info about the park exists, but the New York–based Wildlife Conservation Society helped establish the park and maintains a presence there (*programs.wcs.org/afghanistan*).

• **HOW TO STAY** The city of Bāmyān has a regional airport and a variety of accommodations. A limited number of package tours, such as those offered by Afghan Logistics and Tours (*afghanlogisticstours.com*) or Hinterland Travel (*hinterlandtravel.com*), include stops at the lakes.

PICTURE PERFECT

In the high-altitude, austere valley of Little Pamir, in Afghanistan's far northeastern corner, two crimson-robed Kyrgyz girls retrieve water with the assistance of a Bactrian camel. "It takes two weeks to get to this place," says photographer Matthieu Paley. "A one-week jeep drive from Tajikistan, plus a one-week walk. I slept in a mud house heated by a dry-dung fire." He also points out a detail in this image that's easily missed: "The red veil on top of their hard hats means these Kyrgyz girls are unmarried—once they marry, it will be exchanged [for] a white veil."

IMAGE BY MATTHIEU PALEY
National Geographic photographer

Gangtey Valley

Bhutan's breathtaking and little-known Gangtey Valley is situated on the sun-drenched western slopes of the Black Mountains. Lording over the gently hollowed, treeless valley is the 17th-century cloistered Gangtey Monastery, home to Buddhist monks. Every winter, another population arrives in this sacred valley—elegant black-necked cranes, which migrate south from the Tibetan plateau.

The remote Gangtey Valley (also called Phobjikha Valley) is in the *dzongkhag* (district) of Wangdue Phodrang, and adjacent to the Jigme Singye Wangchuck National Park, a 665-square-mile (1,723 sq km) natural reserve and park that occupies Central Bhutan. Surrounded by looming, densely forested mountains, the glacial valley, sitting at an altitude of 9,840 feet (3,000 m), is a welcome open expanse of wetland, covered mostly by low-growing bamboo and sedge meadow. It's crossed by two rivers, the Nakay Chhu and the Gay Chhu.

The monastery was supposedly founded when Pema Lingpa, a Nyingma saint of Buddhism, saw a hill rising over the low, green floor of the valley and prophesied that a monastery would be built there. His grandson carried through on this vision, and established the monastery in 1613. It is today surrounded by picturesque Gangtey village, inhabited by families that help care for the religious buildings.

The monastery was built in the traditional Tibetan style, and underwent restoration and renovations on its wooden facade and

Mask dances are a highlight of the annual Tsechu religious festivals held in front of the Gangtey Monastery (opposite). In winter, rare black-necked cranes replace Buddhist monks as principal occupants of the valley (above).

Light bathes this glacial valley, tucked into Bhutan's remote Black Mountains.

interior as recently as 2008. At the heart of the religious complex is a *tshokhang,* or prayer hall, one of the largest in Bhutan, decorated with eight pillars and vivid paintings of Buddhist deities and landscapes. Around 100 monks live and work here, all clad in full-length burgundy *gho* robes as they practice meditation and blow traditional trumpetlike horns called *dungchen* during their monastic ceremonies.

As the winter closes in on the Gangtey Valley, the monastery shuts down and the monks retreat to the Wangdue Phodrang

REWIND

National Geographic writer Desmond Doig traveled through the isolated kingdom of Bhutan for three months in 1961 as a guest of King Jigme Dorji Wangchuk. He was the first journalist to set foot in the country, which had been closed to foreigners for centuries. The author and a small group of Indian and Bhutanese nationals traveled 600 miles (966 km) via foot, mule, and horseback on timeworn paths through mountains and valleys. Doig leaned out to capture this shot from above the caravan as it snaked its way up a cliff below the fortress Trongsa Dzong. "A passing mule almost nudged the author to his death," the caption notes matter-of-factly.

By the time this story was getting ready to go to press, the tireless Doig was already off on another far-flung assignment, accompanying Sir Edmund Hillary on an expedition in the Nepalese Himalaya. The story proofs had to be rushed to his campsite at 19,000 feet (5,790 m) by Sherpa runners from Nepal's capital, Kathmandu.

district to wait out the snows that bind the valley until spring. As monks and residents depart, the beautiful, black-necked cranes arrive from their nesting grounds in the north and settle in, foraging among bamboo shoots that livestock have grazed low during the warm months. Elegant and distinctively marked, the birds hold a special place in the hearts of Bhutanese locals. Their haunting, honking calls signal the coming of winter, and legend has it that every year when the cranes return, they circle the monastery three times before landing. Buddhist monks believe these magnificent birds are the reincarnated souls of former lamas, the high priests of Buddhism, and that they return every winter to pay homage to the monastery. So treasured are the birds that for years the residents of the valley forewent

Robes the color of saffron and paprika dry in the sun at the Gangtey Shedra, the monastic school at the Buddhist monastery.

electricity because they feared the wires would entangle the cranes (the valley is connected to the electric grid today with underground cables).

The Black-Necked Crane Information Center is situated on the edge of the forest and wetland along the main road of Gangtey Valley, and has an observation room with spotting scopes, as well as information about the region's natural and cultural history. Several trails cut through the valley and give visitors good vantage points for glimpsing the cranes, not to mention sweeping views of the surrounding Black Mountains.

TRAVELWISE

• **HOW TO VISIT** Visas for Bhutan are relatively easy to obtain, but visitors are required to book their trip through a registered tour operator, included as part of the $200 to $250/day visa fee. Paro is home to the country's only international airport; Druk Air is the national carrier of Bhutan and the only airline that flies into the kingdom (*drukair.com*). Driving and walking are the best ways to get around.

• **PLANNING** Bhutan's Tourism Council offers information about the visa process and details about hiring guides (*tourism.gov.bt/plan/visa*).

• **HOW TO STAY** Amankora, perched on a cliff overlooking Gangtey Valley, offers one of Bhutan's best hot stone baths, and is in earshot of the monastery's Buddhist musicians (*aman.com/resorts/amankora*).

PICTURE
PERFECT

Dozens of prayer flags at Gangtey Monastery flutter about a single flagpole, making a subtle yet eloquent statement against deforestation and logging. "I think the element that struck me most is how simple the concept was and how obvious and effective upon reflection," says photographer Jason Edwards. "That is, fifty prayer flags catching the wind, but exponentially less timber is harvested to display them." He took the image in the late afternoon, so the alpine light was less intense and more forgiving on the flag cloth.

IMAGE BY JASON EDWARDS
National Geographic photographer

Udon Thani

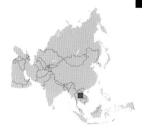

Udon Thani, one of Thailand's 77 provinces, is among the least visited by foreign tourists. The irony is that it shelters one of the world's rare and brilliant phenomena. Each year, during the cool months from December until February, the wetland of Nong Han Kumphawapi turns from a watery green into a showy display of pink lotus blossoms that carpet the lake's tranquil surface.

Twenty-five miles (40 km) away from Udon Thani's eponymous provincial capital, the Nong Han Kumphawapi seems like an ordinary lake for most of the year. Farmers tend to the surrounding rice paddies, and local fishermen paddle out in traditional longboats to cast round nets for fish, and collect delicacies like large snails. Dozens of bird species call this rich habitat home, including the shaggy-plumed gray heron and the eagle-like Brahminy kite.

Beginning in the fall, however, the lake quietly begins to grow an aquatic garden that by December has erupted into full, riotous bloom, the water ablaze with thousands of pink lotuses. From the banks, the wetland's tall elephant grass obscures the lake's pink heart. To appreciate this scene, visitors must hop on a boat that navigates through channels cut through the vegetation by fishers. Then suddenly, the spectacle will reveal itself. Locals may have given this lake the nickname Talay Bua Daeng, or Red Lotus Sea, but the buoyant surface looks more like a meadow, a rich natural tapestry of bold flowers cupped by green, dish-shaped leaves.

The blooms are actually rooted to the wet, mucky mud beneath

Lotus flowers rise above the surface of Nong Han Kumphawapi in the Thai province of Udon Thani. In Wat Pha Phu Kon temple, farther northwest in Udon Thani, a white marble statue of Buddha reclines in sleep (above), a symbol of the largely Buddhist country.

the surface of the shallow water. Their leaves float on the water's surface, while the blooms are held slightly aloft by straight, pale green stalks. Their splashy pink display aside, these flowers have practical uses. They make their way onto food tables, the stems converted into crunchy and spicy salads, and the seeds—which have a light, nutty flavor—a garnish for fish dishes.

The elegant plants also have spiritual resonance: They have come to stand for purity of the mind in Buddhism, as they can thrive and spread beauty even amid the muddiest of waters. This scenic wetland has been nourishing and supporting humankind since the Bronze Age, evidenced by artifacts found in the area. The UNESCO World Heritage site Ban Chiang, an hour northeast of Nong Han Kumphawapi, is considered Southeast Asia's most significant prehistoric settlement, and contains 3,000-year-old farming tools and sophisticated pottery.

The lotus flowers open in the morning sunlight and carpet the lake a deep pink (left). Ancient pottery shards (above) have been discovered at Ban Chiang archaeological site, an hour north of the lake.

▶ TRAVELWISE

• **HOW TO VISIT** Boats launch from the village of Ban Diam in Kumphawapi district, an hour from the city of Udon Thani by train or bus (these will get you to the Kumphawapi district, but you'll need to hire a vehicle for the rest of the trip to Ban Diam). The red lotuses reach their peak between December and February and blossom before 11 a.m. Boats can be hired as early as 6 a.m.

• **PLANNING** The Tourism Authority of Thailand site has general information on visiting the country, including the lake and Ban Chiang (tourism thailand.org). Type in searches for "Kumphawapi" and "Ban Chiang."

• **HOW TO STAY** The 55-room KP Hotel, near Kumphawapi, is humble, but among the nearest accommodations, and costs around $20 a night (219 Moo 9 Udom-samakkee Road).

Huangshan Mountains

For millennia, Chinese poets, artists, and musicians have dedicated their lives to capturing the beauty of the 160-mile-long (257 km) Huangshan massif in China's Anhui Province. Confucian, Taoist, and Buddhist spiritualists have all withdrawn to these mountainous folds in search of reclusion and enlightenment. You too can slip away to discover Huangshan's serene, hidden beauty.

Though Huangshan literally means "Yellow Mountain," the pine-clad granite peaks are anything but sallow. The mountains' current name, which was assigned by an imperial decree in A.D. 747, honors the mythical Yellow Emperor (Huangdi), who is believed to have reigned sometime around the 27th century B.C.

The fog-shrouded peaks are indeed majestic. Romantic monikers like Bright Summit Peak and Lotus Flower Peak mark the tallest of the natural skyscrapers that soar above 6,000 feet (1,829 m). Trails string together a series of peaks, and some visitors spend many days at these heights just admiring the sunrises and sunsets that fall over the rocky valleys and ancient twisted pine trees. At the crack of dawn, rub shoulders with other diligent hikers at Qingliang Tai, and you'll understand why this popular scenic point's name means literally "refreshing terrace" in Chinese. The morning mist clears to reveal staggering rock formations, made famous among the Chinese by traditional art and poetry. Their names are descriptive of their appearance, from Shishu Feng (Stalagmite Peak) to Feilai Shi (Rock Flown From Afar), and even

China's Huangshan mountain range is set off against a morning sky (opposite).
Tibetan macaques, large primates that resemble baboons, live in the high altitudes of these mountains (above).

Mengbi Shenghua (Flower Blooming on the Tip of a Brush). And when you see 5,521-foot (1,682 m) Shixin Feng, below which lives a local species of Tibetan macaques, you might feel the mountain's spiritual aura. Its name, after all, means "beginning to believe peak."

There are three ways to get to the top of these mountains, and each affords a different experience. The eastern ascent, a 5-mile (8 km) hike with shaded paths, is a pleasant walk through Jade Valley, dotted with green pools fed by alpine runoff from Beginning to Believe Peak and other summits. Waterfowl like Mandarin ducks play and mate here, which may have helped the area get its nickname, Lovers' Valley.

Much more strenuous but also more spectacular, the 10-mile (16 km) western ascent is a test of fitness and endurance—seemingly endless stone stairs zigzag up to reveal stellar views at every turn. Man-made structures like pavilions and traditional temples complement the rugged organic crags, and you cross heart-stopping chasms. These natural elements create a vista so romantic that young lovers bring padlocks and metaphorically lock in their love on the railings. And if your legs demand a break, several cable cars provide shortcuts along the way.

The third way to ascend is the easiest—take the cable car all the way.

After you descend, rest your body and soul in Huangshan's popular hot springs. Gushing even during droughts, the 108°F (42°C) water cascades down various falls and feeds the resort area's many pools. As you poach in the soothing water and reflect on the climb, you may find yourself agreeing with the Chinese saying: "You don't need to see any more mountains after seeing the Five Sacred Mountains, but no sacred mountain is worth seeing after you've seen Huangshan."

The peaks and odd formations of Huangshan draw visitors in all seasons, including winter, which lasts from around October to March.

▶ TRAVELWISE

• **HOW TO VISIT** Huangshan receives much rain, especially during the wet months from June to August. The temperature drops quickly as you ascend, so dress warmly and prepare for fog any time of the year. Fall is considered the most pleasant time to visit. The town of Tunxi, an hour away by bus, provides the closest base. The city of Hangzhou is 3.5 hours away with frequent bus services.

• **PLANNING** The China National Tourism Office provides information on the region (cnto.org).

• **HOW TO STAY** Hotels of all price categories dot the mountain ranges. The 180-room Xihai Hotel is at the foot of Danxia Peak (www.hsxihai hotel.cn/en/index.html).

PICTURE
PERFECT

Wind and water over centuries whittled and polished the vertiginous landscape of Wulingyuan Scenic and Historic Interest Area, located about 600 miles (965 km) east of Huangshan in Hunan Province. The glass Bailong (or Hundred Dragons) elevator in the photo brings visitors more than 1,000 feet (305 m) to the top of the cliffs. Fans of the movie *Avatar* will recognize these floating peaks as the fictional world of Pandora. "Even without the help of CGI and 3-D, it's easy to see why *Avatar*'s set designers chose Wulingyuan," said photographer Michael Yamashita. "Its scenery is amazing."

IMAGE BY MICHAEL YAMASHITA
National Geographic photographer

TAIWAN

North Coast

A bizarre, beautiful landscape lies beyond the northern outskirts of Taiwan's capital city, Taipei. Known as the North Coast and Guanyinshan National Scenic Area, this region extends from the west bank of the Tamsui River east to Keelung on Taiwan's northern coast. The Daliesque rock formations, crashing waves, volcanic mountains, and hot springs have a wild, fantastical quality.

Both parts of this region are worth exploring. The larger, water-focused North Coast is busy on midsummer weekends, but week-days are less crowded. The stretch of the North Coast from Tamsui east to Keelung is historically known as the Jumping Stone Coast, and with good reason. Before the shore-hugging roads were con-structed, people would scramble over boulders to travel between coastal areas.

The crown jewels of the Jumping Stone rock collection are found in Yehliu Geopark, a natural fairyland of sedimentary rock formations and sea caves sculpted over millennia by the sea, waves, wind, and sun. Many of the rock formations are named for things they loosely resemble—such as Queen's Head and Beehive—and all are off-limits to climbers to help protect the landscape from human-caused erosion. Off-season is the prime time to experience the primeval park at its wildest. Those willing to brave the ele-ments—including possible wind, rain, and cold temperatures—are treated to thundering waves, swirling cloud formations, and the solitude and serenity of a deserted beach.

The North Coast of Taiwan encompasses the weird rock formations of Yehliu Geological Park (opposite).
Many have taken on distinctive forms, including these that look like honeycombed mushrooms (above).

Farther to the west, the Laomei Green Reef is a magnificent sight that seems almost too vivid and sculptural to be natural. Over the years, volcanic lava was abraded by waves into long, sinuous fingers that extend into the East China Sea. In April and May, algae grows on these reefs and carpets them a brilliant green, set off by the white spray of surf as the tidal waters flood around them.

The North Coast is famous for its hot springs. The geologically active region is particularly known for its variety of geothermal waters, and temperatures generally range between 95 and 136°F (35 to 58°C), depending on location. Top hot spring destinations include Beitou (where the waters are thought to have healing powers); coastal Jinshan, which offers the irresistible combination of steaming hot waters and cool sea views; and Yangmingshan National Park, home to a number of hot springs areas that can be reached via biking or hiking trails.

The Guanyinshan part of the scenic area is smaller, and centered on an extinct volcano called Guanyinshan. Legend has it that Guanyinshan is named for Guanyin, the Chinese Buddhist goddess of mercy, kindness, and compassion. The region's volcanic mountain range, from a distance, supposedly looks somewhat like Guanyin reclined in sleep.

Several well-marked hiking trails lead through Guanyinshan's bamboo forests and grassy meadows, and from February to March, past blooming cherry trees and azaleas. Bird-watchers flock here in the spring and fall to see migratory birds, including raptors such as the crested serpent eagle *(Spilornis cheela),* the Asian crested goshawk *(Accipiter trivirgatus),* and the gray-faced buzzard *(Butastur indicus).* Hike up to 2,021-foot (616-m) Yinghanling—Guanyinshan's highest peak—for sweeping views of Taipei, the mountains, the sea, the Tamsui River, and the historic port town of Tamsui.

Surf pours around the algae-blanketed lava fingers of Laomei Green Reef, visible at low tide. The color is most striking in April and May.

▶ TRAVELWISE

- **HOW TO VISIT** Ride the Taipei MRT (Metro) to Tamsui. From Tamsui Wharf, hop a ferry for the 10-minute ride to Bali, gateway to Guanyinshan Mountain. Return to Tamsui, and buy a one-day pass aboard a tourist shuttle. The hop-on, hop-off tourist bus connects major attractions on Provincial Highway 2, the scenic coastal route between Tamsui and Keelung.

- **PLANNING** A couple sites provide travel information for the region *(www.northguan-nsa.gov.tw; www.taiwantrip.com.tw).*

- **WHERE TO GO** Luxuriate in an outdoor hot spring pool in the shadow of the mountains or in a private (in-room) hot spring bath at the Yangmingshan Tien Lai Resort & Spa *(tienlai.com.tw).*

PICTURE PERFECT

"Taipei is a fascinating location to shoot as it is a real mix of traditional and Chinese culture," says photographer Sean Gallagher. Perhaps no place sums it up better than Mengjia Longshan Temple in the heart of Taipei. Radiating an aura of gold, Taiwan's oldest temple teems with worshippers, spiritual offerings, and thick swirls of incense. Inside, a statue of Guanyin, the goddess of mercy, takes center stage, though in this multidenominational temple, originally founded by Han immigrants from Fujian in 1738, hundreds of other deities are celebrated as well.

IMAGE BY SEAN GALLAGHER
National Geographic photographer

Batanes

The northernmost reach of the Filipino archipelago is a clutch of 10 small islands that make up the province of Batanes, between Taiwan and the Philippine's main island, Luzon. Only three of these islands are settled, and with a robust fishing culture, limestone architecture, pristine landscape, and a general lack of crowds, they are a destination unlike any other in the Pacific.

On the main island of Batan, which is roughly half the size of Brooklyn, a neck of land tapers to about a mile (1.6 km) at its narrowest point and connects two volcanoes: the modest and inactive Mount Matarem, and the cloud-clipped, 3,310-foot (1,009 m) Mount Iraya, which last erupted in 1454. Though innocently cloaked in greenery today, it has a crater almost a mile wide (1.6 km) and is still an active volcano. Nearly two millennia ago it had a fiery outburst that spewed andesite rocks over the northern half of the island: The result was Valugan Beach, a rocky shoreline bordered by cliffs and coconut trees, and composed of boulders that have been smoothed by centuries of lapping sapphire waves.

Yet it's not seismic activity that makes the trees sway here, but legendary gales of wind. Cool, mighty gusts batter Vayang hills on the northwestern edge of Batan, and hikers on the ridge can be seen crouching to regain their balance. Lean, sure-footed cattle, on the other hand, trot nimbly across the farmland and graze by hedgerows, totally unperturbed by the blasting currents of air. Pacific means "peaceable," but the ocean here is anything but. Wild

The restful green slopes of Mount Iraya (opposite) belie its status as an active volcano. Shuttle boats (above) ferry people and supplies from island to island in the Batanes archipelago of the Philippines.

The Tukon Chapel on the island of Basco overlooks the West Philippine Sea.

grass shimmers on rolling hills that give away to dramatic cliffs, and down below, the ocean roils against the coastline.

Landscape aside, Batanes is an escape from the seething, distrustful urban sprawl of the modern world. The people of the islands, the Ivatan, are an ethnic group of uncertain origin and are known to be trusting and good-natured. Bicycle around the island of Batan on the serpentine, single-track National Road, and you will likely find every driver and bicyclist you meet greets you with a nod and a smile. At the airport, the gates stay open to let livestock pass—except when propeller planes land once or twice a day.

The Ivatan have their own language and developed rituals and symbols unique to their island culture. They once interred their dead with pre-Spanish stone burial markers, shaped like a boat with bows and sterns, and scholars believe these may have been aligned to the Milky Way. The extravagant cultural rites aren't confined to the deceased. In the fishing hamlet of Diura on the eastern shore, a solemn ritual is conducted each March at the start of the fishing season. A haruspex (officiant) sacrifices a pig and inspects its organs to predict how abundant the year's catch will be. After offering the pig's blood to the sea to ensure safe journeys, the fishermen brave the rough waves in wooden boats. The dorado fish (also known as mahimahi) is the prized catch.

Near another inhabited island called Sabtang, jumping pods of dolphins might cross paths with the wooden *faluwa* vessels

Beachcombers enjoy the open expanses of the islands' shorelines. Batanes is lightly populated—in fact, only three of its islands are inhabited at all.

This photo, by Army pilot Lieutenant G. W. Goddard, accompanied a *National Geographic* story on a mapmaking expedition in the Philippines by the U.S. Army's Sixth Photographic Section. In the late 1920s, this unit was assigned to fly over and photograph a stretch of northeast Luzon that was still uncharted territory for the U.S. government.

Goddard's team used de Havilland bombers (pictured, above northern Luzon mountains) and Loening seaplanes to shoot survey images of the terrain at 12,000 feet (3,658 m). One of the bombers was outfitted with a collapsible dark room that allowed photographers to develop images mid-flight in about eight minutes, so they could ensure their footage was effective.

Flying in the tropics in primitive aircraft could be harrowing. At one point, Goddard's engine started stalling, and he looked down to see 20-foot (6 m) swells beating the coastline below him—"It looked like suicide to try them in a land plane." Just as he began to panic, his engine picked up and he made it safely back to his base.

Women also use it to fashion *vakul*, a headgear that resembles a long, voluminous wig and keeps off the rain.

Sabtang's sheer cliffs have a rugged yet fragile beauty and are footed by inviting coves and deserted beaches. The Ivatan used the rocky outcrops called *idjang* as fortresses until 18th-century Spanish conquerors arrived.

TRAVELWISE

• **HOW TO VISIT** March through May brings the warmest and least windy weather. The islands can be accessed only by air, and Philippine Airlines and low-cost SkyJet connect Basco, capital city of Batan, with Manila.

• **PLANNING** The Philippine Department of Tourism publishes travel information for Batanes (*itsmorefuninthephilippines.com/batanes*).

• **HOW TO STAY** Fundacion Pacita is the only upscale accommodation on Batan, affording a panorama of rolling hills and the West Philippine Sea from luxurious rooms in Basco (*fundacionpacita.ph*). The town has numerous other basic and clean hotels from around $20.

carrying passengers and sacks of green bananas. With around 1,600 residents living in a few sleepy villages scattered around 12.5 square miles (32 sq km), Sabtang is even more rustic than Batan. Hardy fishermen and farmers live in traditional homes of limestone studded with fossils in the village of Savidug, named after the local word for the sea almond trees that grow abundantly there. Houses are roofed with fuzzy *voyavoy* palm leaves that somehow withstand even hurricanes. This palm fiber is a versatile material:

PICTURE PERFECT

Ivatan children play near a wave-thrashed pier on the hard-to-reach island of Itbayat, part of the Batanes archipelago province. Photographer Hannah Reyes braved a rough cargo boat ride to this island. "I found myself seated beside a cow on the four-hour ride," she says, "as I double-checked that all my equipment was sealed from the water." Once there, Reyes found this carefree scene captivating. "On top of diving, the boys were playing catch with their slippers," she says. "My favorite miniscule detail in this photograph is the slipper near the boy in the green shirt."

IMAGE BY HANNAH REYES
National Geographic photographer

Bohol Island Chocolate Hills

The conical Chocolate Hills of Bohol Island in the Philippines are a mystery of nature. The estimated 1,776 grass-covered, coral limestone karst domes are nearly uniform in shape, with a smooth, symmetrical geometry. Adding to their intrigue is the fact that their name—Chocolate Hills—is something of a misnomer because lush foliage paints the mounds a vibrant, emerald green for much of the year.

These mounds are not anthills—they range between 40 to 260 feet (12 to 80 m) tall, and one outlier inexplicably towers 390 feet (119 m), about the height of a 30-story building. It's only in the driest months (typically March to May) that the Chocolate Hills somewhat match their popular moniker. With little rain, the grass on the hills turns a golden brown, making the mounds resemble massive haystacks. Add a healthy dose of imagination, and the rain-starved landscape could even be row upon row of giant chocolate drops.

Whether green or brown, the Chocolate Hills are a topographical anomaly found only on Bohol Island. Unlike other famous groupings of conical karsts—such as the limestone hills of Java's Gunung Sewu ("thousand mountains") region in Indonesia—the Bohol mounds are so perfectly rounded that they seem almost unnatural. Creation myths connected to the hills include one popular legend that the mounds are clutter created by two sparring giants who fought with stones and sand. Another tale says the hills sprang from the tears of a giant following the death of his human lover.

Sunrise bathes the Chocolate Hills—hundreds and hundreds of them—with a gentle golden light (opposite).
Inland, the Tarsier Sanctuary protects the world's smallest (and probably most bug-eyed) primates (above).

This aerial photograph was taken by U.S. Army Air Corps Lieutenant Lloyd Barnett, Jr. in around 1944, during World War II. It shows a fishing village northwest of the northern Bohol town of Talibon, surrounded on three sides by the Camotes Sea. The image was pulled from the National Geographic archives, but despite its striking perspective, it has never been published. The precise village shown in this shot is not identified, but what is certain is that its inhabitants, and all the inhabitants of Bohol Island, were in the midst of some tumultuous years.

The Japanese had invaded Bohol Island in 1944, and the Filipino people had organized guerrilla movements to resist their occupiers. These guerrilla forces harassed and unnerved the Japanese, and were a significant help to the American forces that arrived to liberate the Visayan Islands from the Japanese in the spring of 1945. When American troops got to Bohol in April, the guerrilla forces helped them push inland and clear the island of Japanese resistance.

A less whimsical theory holds that the hills were created by water and wind eroding layers of limestone rock, sitting on a base of impermeable clay. However, there is no real scientific consensus on the formation of the Hills, and by and large their origin remains shaded in mystery. On one thing, everyone agrees: For the hills to have been a man-made endeavor would have involved an effort so monumental that it is highly, highly unlikely.

The Chocolate Hills are visible throughout the towns of Carmen, Batuan, and Sagbayan in Bohol's jungle interior. To help protect the domes from mining and development, the Philippine government designated the Chocolate Hills as a National Geological Monument in 1988. (Rice cultivation and small-scale farming are permitted on the flats between the hills.) In addition, the Chocolate Hills Natural Monument is part of the "Tentative List" recommended for inclusion in the UNESCO World Heritage site list.

Some of the highest 360-degree views of the hills are from the top deck of the government-run Chocolate Hills Complex in Carmen. The 2013 Bohol earthquake damaged parts of the viewing platform here, so watch your steps—all 200-plus of them—on the way to the top.

Soaring over the hills is possible at the newer Chocolate Hills Adventure Park, also in Carmen. The privately owned park is a tad touristy, but look past the kitsch to focus on the panoramic vistas of the Chocolate Hills seen from the park's signature attraction, Bike Zip. This combination cycling/zip lining ride follows a double-cable path strung 150 feet (45 m) above the ground. For a more down-to-earth perspective (literally), camp overnight in the park to see the Chocolate Hills bathed in orange light at sunrise and sunset.

Women work in rice fields at the foot of the "Chocolate" Hills, which are actually lush and green for much of the year.

The Chocolate Hills aren't the only natural oddity of this region. On your way to see them, stop off and visit the nonprofit Philippine Tarsier Foundation's Tarsier Sanctuary near Corella *(tarsierfounda tion.org)*. The small reserve offers the rare opportunity to watch the tiny tarsier (the heaviest tip the scales at 5 ounces/142 g), a nocturnal primate, sleeping in its natural habitat, clinging to a tree. The animal is endemic to the Philippines and each of its giant, glassy, protuberant eyes is roughly the size and weight of its little brain.

> **TRAVELWISE**

- **HOW TO VISIT** Take a fast ferry from Cebu City to Bohol's Tagbilaran City tourist pier. From here, rent a motorbike, or hire a jeepney to get to the main Chocolate Hills Complex in Carmen. Several Bohol tour operators also offer guided Chocolate Hills day trips *(Islandrentals.ph)*.

- **PLANNING** Several sites have travel info *(boholtourismph.com; itsmorefuninthephilippines.com; chocolatehillsadventurepark.com)*.

- **HOW TO STAY** Refurbished in 2015, Nuts Huts is a rustic ecolodge with basic wood bungalows *(nutshuts.org)*.

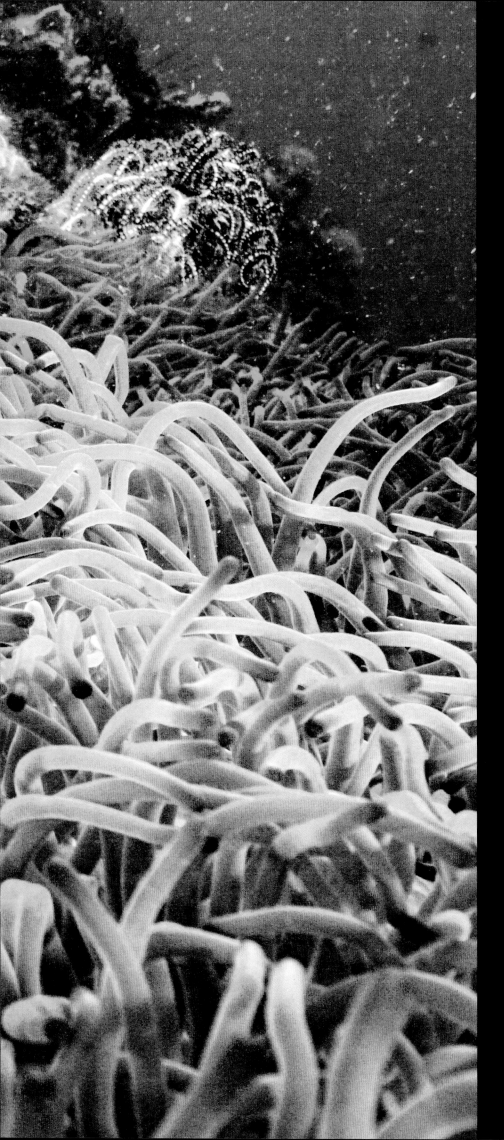

PICTURE
PERFECT

Photographer Tim Laman captured this image of two false clown anemonefish swimming around tentacled sea anemones in the clear waters off Malapascua Island in the Philippine province of Cebu. "Anemonefish are very photogenic," says Laman, "but are constantly moving, darting around their anemone. I found that the trick to getting a nice composition is to get in position and then wait for the fish to arrange themselves in a pleasing position—then quickly take the shot." He points out that if you look closely, you can see several more fish in this photo, mostly hidden in the anemone.

IMAGE BY TIM LAMAN
National Geographic photographer

Icebergs drift in the
frigid waters of Antarctica's
Weddell Sea.

Australia, South Pacific, & Antarctica

Rain forests, watery grottoes, islands of penguins and kangaroos, and icebergs the size of a city—these are the wonders of Australia and Oceania.

Daintree Rainforest

Daintree Rainforest, in the wet tropics of far north Queensland, is the oldest rain forest in the world. In this tropical jungle wilderness, giant reptiles, flightless birds, and other living fossils lurk in the shadows, while a tangle of shrubs, vines, and palms stretch skyward for sunlight. Neither ancient nor modern, Daintree is an ever-evolving wonder of the world.

A mere 20 minutes north of the coastal city of Port Douglas, the clamor of civilization gives way to birdsong, the trilling of tree frogs, and the fluttering of Ulysses butterflies. Daintree's 2 million-plus acres (more than 800,000 ha) of rain forest, estuaries, mangroves, beaches, eucalypt forests, and hinterland support roughly a third of all mammals and over half the bird species found in Australia.

At the top of the rain forest food chain sits the toothy saltwater crocodile, patrolman of the area's mangroves and open waters.

Crocs are best observed from the safety of a Daintree River cruise boat—needless to say, swimming in salt water, including tidal rivers, is highly inadvisable.

The Daintree's second most famous resident is the southern cassowary, a large flightless bird native to New Guinea and this northernmost spindle of Australia. It's a striking creature, with shiny black feathers, an indigo neck, two dangling red wattles, and a distinctive bony helmet called a casque crowning its head. The adult females can reach up to 6 feet (1.8 m), though males remain

The lagoons and forests of Mossman Gorge (opposite) shelter the dainty tree frog (above), one of a huge number of plants and animals that thrive in the warm, moist environs of Daintree Rainforest.

slightly smaller and are primary caregivers for chicks. As the Daintree's self-appointed farmers, cassowaries eat fruit and redistribute seeds too large for other animals to ingest.

A relic of Daintree's past is the unfortunately named idiot fruit *(Idiospermum australiense),* a 110-million-year-old species appropriately nicknamed the "green dinosaur." This extremely rare and primitive flowering plant, probably once fodder for megafauna, is toxic to the rain forest's animals today. With cassowaries to scatter its seeds, the idiot fruit has survived in undisturbed pockets of lowland rain forest, aided only by gravity in its seed dispersal.

By contrast, humans have inhabited the region for a mere 40,000 years. The forest's traditional custodians, the aboriginal Kuku Yalanji, lead "dreamtime gorge walks" along the Mossman River, past moss-covered boulders, sandy banks, and waterfalls.

You can visit Daintree any time of year, though different seasons bring different challenges. Summer rains and monsoons fill rivers, waterfalls, and swimming holes, but can also wash out roads. Winter brings more comfortable temperatures, but you'll also find the rain forest at its height of tourist congestion.

A saltwater crocodile patrols the banks of the Daintree River (above). Daintree Rainforest covers more than 2 million acres (nearly 900,000 ha) and runs into the beaches of Cape Tribulation (right).

▶ TRAVELWISE

• **HOW TO VISIT** From Port Douglas, car itineraries head north on paved roads to Mossman Gorge, across the Daintree River by car ferry, and through the jungle to Cape Tribulation. The drive takes two hours.

• **PLANNING** Several sites have good resources *(discoverthedaintree .com; whc.unesco.org/en/list/486; daintreerainforest.net.au).*

• **HOW TO STAY** Besides camping, the cheapest overnight is at the Daintree Rainforest Observatory where visitors sleep free in exchange for volunteer work *(research.jcu.edu.au/dro/experiences/volunteering).* On the higher end, Silky Oaks Lodge offers luxury accommodation along the Mossman River *(silkyoakslodge.com.au).*

Phillip Island

A 2,100-foot (640 m) bridge connects the south coast of mainland Australia to the farming community of Phillip Island. Cross it and you find yourself in a world of sandy beaches and mild weather, where you can spot koalas in the treetops and see penguins on parade. With its rugged coastline, the island is a summertime destination for sunbathers, bird-watchers, fishermen, and surfers.

Cape Woolamai—a headland at the southeastern tip of Phillip Island—is the first stop on a loop of the 39-square-mile (100 sq km) island. Barring summer traffic, the circuit can be done in an hour, but the pink granite cliffs and wide beaches of Woolamai are usually enough to persuade a visitor that's not enough time. A series of walking trails wind along beaches and cliff tops to the island's highest point. From here, there are panoramic views across the Bass Strait and the ocean-carved granite towers that rise out of it.

From Cape Woolamai, the road turns inland, toward the Koala Conservation Centre, where you can stroll through the eucalyptus leaves on elevated, treetop boardwalks and get an up-close look at Australia's sweet-looking, faux bears. The endangered creatures are actually marsupials, and if you're lucky, you might see a baby koala venturing out of its mother's pouch—the young animals hitch a ride on their mother until they're a year old. Besides the koalas, the whole of Phillip Island is alive with Australia's iconic wildlife, so keep your eyes peeled at all times for kangaroos and wallabies,

Water and wind sculpted the pink granite rock formations known as the Pinnacles at Cape Woolamai, Phillip Island's highest point (opposite). A shy koala bear (above) peers at visitors from a tree at the Koala Conservation Centre.

A boardwalk winds over Point Grant toward the Nobbies on the western tip of Phillip Island.

and scan the waters for singing whales and hungry pelicans.

Heading west through the island's rural inland, you come to Summerland, a modern ghost town, though you won't know it from looking. It was once home to a buzzing residential community of which there is little trace today. Starting in the 1980s, the regional government thought better of the development, bought up the houses, took them down, and restored the peninsula for the island's preeminent residents: *Eudyptula minor,* the little penguins.

At sunset, Phillip Island's penguins return from the waters of the Bass Strait, where they swim and forage for up to several weeks at a time. They toddle across the sandy beaches and huddle into burrows in the ground, where they take refuge from harsh weather,

rest, nest, or depending on the season, feed their young. The little penguins choose dusk as their hour to come ashore because it offers them protection from predators. More than 4,000 of them—some just a foot tall—gather on Summerland Beach, a spectacle humans have fondly dubbed the "Penguin Parade." Phillip Island Nature Park offers several options for viewing this event: The "ultimate adventure" package includes night vision scopes and a hike through the penguin colony. And when you're done watching the endearing birds waddle en masse to their burrows, turn your eyes skyward. The night sky here is inky black, and the Southern Cross constellation, once an important navigation point, glows vividly on clear nights.

A wallaby hops along **Summerland Peninsula**, once a residential development. It was reclaimed as a part of **Phillip Island Nature Park**.

This photo of a keeper lighting Cape Jaffa Lighthouse in South Australia was shot in 1970, during *National Geographic* editor Howell Walker's travels through the state. Back then, the lighthouse was located offshore on Margaret Brock Reef, and a lighthouse keeper lit its kerosene wicks every night to warn ships away from the dangerous currents. The keepers and their families—sometimes up to three at a time—lived in the quarters at the base of the lighthouse. Shortly after Walker's visit, the Cape Jaffa Lighthouse was decommissioned after a century of service and was physically moved a few miles northeast to Kingston, where it now sits on dry land and is a museum.

This was not Walker's first trip to Australia. In 1941, National Geographic had sent him there on a six-month reporting jaunt—and he'd ended up staying for five and a half years, fighting World War II with the United States Army Air Forces in Australia, New Guinea, and the Pacific.

bask, swim, and dive for fish off these rocky outcrops. You can head to the island's biggest town, Cowes, and hop on an ecocruise for a more immediate perspective on these flippered mammals. They playfully surround the boats, bobbing about spiritedly. Complete your tour of Phillip Island by heading east back toward the mainland along roads that may find you slowing down to allow kangaroos to cross.

▶ TRAVELWISE

- **HOW TO VISIT** Phillip Island is just a 90-minute drive from Melbourne. The holiday season is the busiest time of year; if you plan to visit between mid-December and mid-January, book tickets for events like the Penguin Parade well in advance.

- **PLANNING** You'll find information and general planning resources at a couple good sites (*visitphillipisland.com; penguins.org.au*).

- **HOW TO STAY** Phillip Island is small enough for a one-day tour and picturesque enough for a leisurely stay in one of the island's quaint seaside bed-and-breakfasts. The island is also dotted with caravan parks for the many who choose to camp or RV.

At the very western tip of the Summerland Peninsula, you reach the Nobbies, a rugged segment of the coastline where massive boulders rise out of the tidal waters just offshore. A boardwalk and walking paths allow for an easy amble along the sea bluffs. They bring you to a great vantage point on a blowhole, a sea cave 40 feet (12 m) deep. When strong southern swells rush into this cavity, the blowhole returns a forceful jet spray from the mouth of the cave.

Farther off the coast, one of the continent's largest colonies of fur seals lives at Seal Rocks, and the social creatures frolic, wallow,

PICTURE PERFECT

Bright, midday light contrasts the shadowy interior of a cave, just off the coast of Adelaide, Australia, with the sun-drenched coastline. "A lot of photographers might have considered this bad light," says photographer Amy Toensing, who was in Australia working on a story about the continent's extinct megafauna. "But it created this incredible dramatic shadow." She and her husband were on a pressed schedule when she took this photo, and she almost left without getting the shot. "My husband insisted I crawl into this space before we left. I'm glad I let myself be persuaded!"

IMAGE BY AMY TOENSING
National Geographic photographer

Birds of Paradise

Sitting smack on top of the volatile Pacific Ring of Fire, Papua New Guinea is home to active volcanoes that erupt with enough force to disperse clouds. The island is blanketed with steamy tropical rain forests that teem with life, and among its most interesting inhabitants are 38 species of birds of paradise, dazzling, iridescent creatures known for their flamboyant mating rituals.

The New Guinea Highlands, also known as the Central Range or Central Cordillera, bisect the world's second largest island from east to west, while a political boundary runs north to south, dividing the island into Indonesia on the western side and Papua New Guinea in the east. Papua New Guinea and its 600-some islands are home to skull caves, coral reefs, diveable wrecks, atolls, and so many indigenous tribes and clans that the country is considered one of the most culturally diverse in the world. At least 836 languages are spoken here—but the one fervently sought after by many visitors is the haunting call of the endemic and colorful birds of paradise.

The resplendent birds are found from the hill forests of Fergusson Island in Milne Bay to the rain-forested foothills of the Morobe Province on the northeastern coast. But the highest number of species is concentrated in the rugged Papua Highlands. Here, in the dense casuarina groves of the Adelbert Range, the superb bird of paradise (*Lophorina superba*) lives—and tries energetically to mate. The male birds have a distinctive teal breast shield that stands

out like a third wing. When the birds come courting, this breast shield is wielded in one of the most bizarre, transfixing displays of passion you can hope to see. The male lifts a black cape of feathers into a broad cuff that stands out around its head, and projects its teal breast shield so that all that's visible to the female is what appears to be a leering turquoise face. This position assumed, the male hops around in a frenzied jig that only a female of its own species could find alluring.

Farther south, in the Owen Stanley Range, known for its lush and remote razor-backed ridges, you will find more subtle—but no less strange—forms of this ritual. The brilliantly colored blue birds of paradise (*Paradisaea rudolphi*) have long, streaming tail feathers that look like ribbons. They hang upside down from a branch with these tendrils dangling down about their heads, and flutter their wings wide in a display they hope is irresistible to a mate.

The millinery trade of the late 19th and early 20th centuries significantly decreased the populations of these gorgeous and peculiar birds, but as a result, all species of birds of paradise in Papua New Guinea are now protected. Removing their plume from

A vividly colored male blue bird of paradise looks for his next conquest from a fruit tree in the southern highlands.

In this 1917 photo from the National Geographic archives, workers stand amid the tamed rows of an 8,000-acre (3,240 ha) coconut plantation in Papua New Guinea's southern Milne Bay Province. Dried coconut kernels called copra are still one of the country's chief agricultural exports, but a decade after this photo was taken, the U.S. Department of Agriculture had become interested in a different Papuan crop.

The department sponsored a National Geographic expedition by seaplane into the country's remote interior in around 1929 to find new types of sugarcane, in the hopes of uncovering a more disease-resistant strain. Though the team returned to Washington, D.C. from the 200-day venture with 130 new cane varieties, they were far more impressed by Papua's diverse tribal communities. "Primarily, of course, we came for cane," wrote expedition leader E. W. Brandes, "Yet . . . it was only natural that the strange tribes we bartered with were even more interesting than the plant life we found."

This tropical environment supports an incredibly rich array of wildlife, and it isn't just the birds that widen eyes—in the Oro Province, on the eastern edge of Papua New Guinea, the largest butterfly in the world, the Queen Alexandra's birdwing, can have a wingspan of nearly a foot (30 cm).

▶ TRAVELWISE

• **HOW TO VISIT** Papua New Guinea's main airport is Jacksons International in the city of Port Moresby, which has direct links to Manila, Hong Kong, Singapore, Sydney, Tokyo, and Brisbane. Because there are few paved roads, the country is heavily reliant on aviation to access remote parts of the highlands. The best months for birding are during the dry season from June to October.

• **PLANNING** For more information, check out Papua New Guinea Tourism's excellent website, which includes its own birds of paradise field guide (*papuanewguinea.travel/birdwatching*).

• **HOW TO STAY** Cox & Kings offers a nine-day tour of the Papua New Guinea Highlands that engages with local tribes and highlights birds of paradise. These tours offer on-the-ground local guides and stays at bird lodges like Karawari Lodge and Ambua Lodge (*coxandkingsusa.com*).

the country is forbidden, but even so, logging and decimation of their habitat remains a serious threat to the birds.

Even beyond the birds of paradise, this part of the world is remote and beautiful. The island in its entirety is a land of opposites—a glacier crowns its tallest heights, on the summit of Puncak Jaya mountain on the Indonesian side, while average temperatures can hover around 90°F (32°C) at sea level in the warmer months.

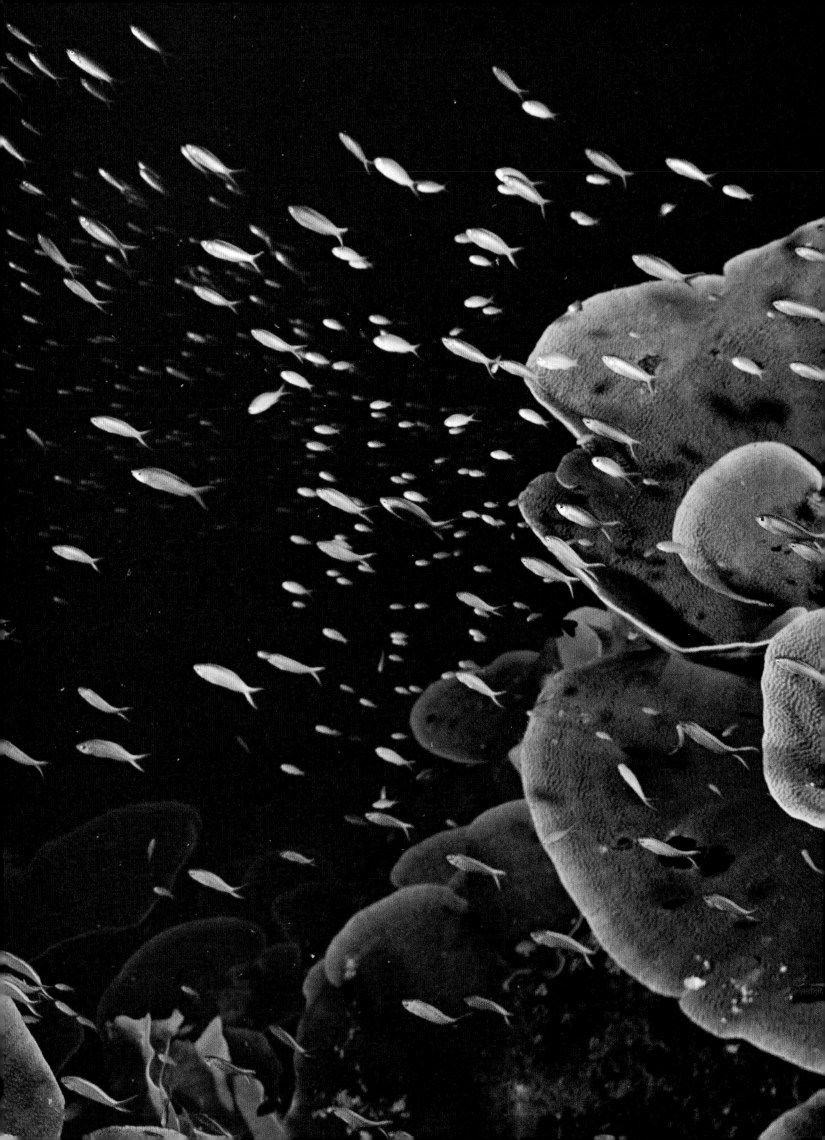

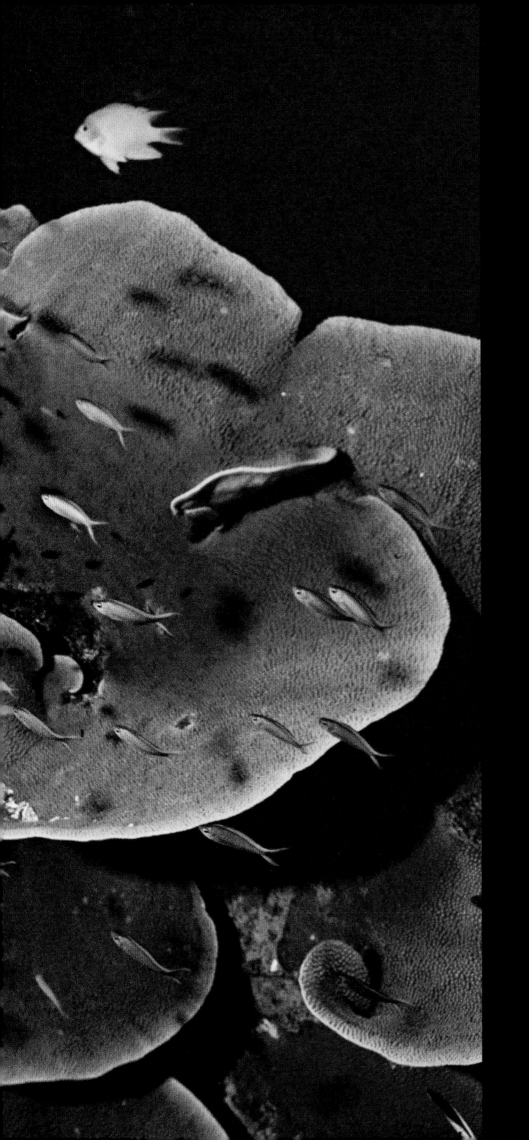

PICTURE
PERFECT

In tropical waters teeming with more than a thousand species of coral and two thousand species of reef fish, purple anthiases and yellow damselfish stream past beautifully sculptured chalice coral in Papua New Guinea's Milne Bay. Famed for his underwater images, photographer David Doubilet claims he has spent more than half his life submerged since taking his first underwater photograph at age eight.

IMAGE BY DAVID DOUBILET
National Geographic photographer

Waitomo Glowworm Caves

A boat glides silently along the Waitomo River; all is darkness as the waterway winds through ancient limestone caves. Suddenly, deep below ground, a twinkling galaxy appears overhead. This is not the night sky, but tens of thousands of *Arachnocampa luminosa*—glowworms with an eerie blue-green luminescence—suspended in the Waitomo Glowworm Grotto.

On the North Island of New Zealand, a system of caves and rivers burrow their way through the soft limestone beneath green, rolling topography. The most famous of these caves—the Glowworm Grotto—was a legend among the local Maori people by the time it was first extensively explored by a Maori chief and an English surveyor in 1887. By 1889, the limestone caves and the glowworms (which are actually not worms at all, but larval fungus gnats found only in parts of New Zealand and Australia) had become a tourist destination. More than 125 years later, the glowing insects remain a source of wonderment for visitors. Their light gives the impression they are larger, but each glowworm is in fact smaller than a mosquito.

The glowworms—or larval gnats, if you must—are drawn to the caves where they are protected from air currents that might interfere with their unique method of procuring food. A single glowworm suspends from the cave ceiling dozens of long, silky fishing lines sticky with mucus. Attracted by the light of the glowworms, insects fly toward the cave ceiling and become ensnared in this

Near Waitomo, the limestone arches of Mangapohue Natural Bridge (opposite) are left over from a collapsed cave system. The Waitomo Glowworm Grotto (above) is famous for caverns that look like starry night skies.

deadly suspended net. What a visitor sees is much more romantic: a shimmering, delicate fringe of silky threads suspended from the cavern ceiling.

Beyond the Glowworm Grotto is a maze of caves. The dramatic Tomo shaft, carved out by a long-forgotten waterfall, plunges more than 50 feet (15 m) into the earth; in the enormous "Cathedral" the forces of nature have crafted a cavern with superb acoustics; a choir sings in the cave 295 feet (90 m) underground each Christmas season. Nearby Aranui Cave's ceiling drips with pink, brown, and white stalactites formed over millions of years.

Most visitors to the region explore the limestone formations on foot and by boat, a leisurely wander through a museum of unrivaled natural craftsmanship. Others go "black water rafting" in Ruakuri Cave, an adventure that can include a slow and serene trip by inner tube through the Glowworm Grotto.

The eerie blue "stars" of the Glowworm Grotto are actually larval gnats trying to attract bugs they can ensnare and eat (above). In Lost Cave, part of Waitomo caves, visitors rappel into a cavern (opposite).

▶ TRAVELWISE

• **HOW TO VISIT** The Waitomo Glowworm Caves are a popular summer destination. Reserve tickets in advance and arrive on time for your tour. The caves are about 122 miles (196 km) from Auckland, and many bus tours from the city include the caves on their itineraries.

• **PLANNING** Book tickets for cave tours online (*waitomo.com*).

• **HOW TO STAY** Waitomo has numerous hotels to accommodate visitors. The storybook Waitomo Caves Hotel was one of the first. The grand hotel was built in 1908 to house the first waves of visitors to the Glowworm Grotto (*waitomocaveshotel.co.nz*).

Bay of Fires

Tasmania's Bay of Fires is a dazzling sight—a turquoise green sea fringed by white sands, all backed by blood orange, lichen-encrusted granite headlands. With an ancient history of geologic activity and a more recent history of Aboriginal occupation, this pristine shore on Tasmania's remote northeastern tip is home to Australia's celebrated wildlife and dramatic, coastal scenery.

Some 380 million years ago, a period of plate collision and mountain building formed this landscape. Belowground, volcanic heat produced magma that formed large crystals as it cooled. The resulting granite eventually made its way to the surface, and broke down purely into beautiful white beaches, but very poor soils. Dubbed the Tasmanian Serengeti, a scrubland of sand dunes and heath borders the bay and is home to Australia's "big five" (wild animals, that is): kangaroo, Tasmanian devil, wombat, platypus, and quoll.

"Bay of Fires" actually does not refer to the orange hue of the rocks. The name dates from 1773, when English Captain Tobias Furneaux was traveling along the coast and spotted the campfires of the Aboriginals residing in the region. Today, strolling along the beach, you'll likely still see middens (shell and bone deposits) from that time.

The Bay of Fires comprises three separate sections, south to north, and all look much as they did when Furneaux first spotted the Aboriginal fires, complete with white-breasted sea eagles and gannets gliding on the ocean air. The southern section, located near the outposts of St. Helens and Binalong Bay, is the easiest to access. The coast here stretches about 8 miles (13 km) between Binalong Bay and the Gardens and is preserved as the Bay of Fires Conservation Area. An especially magnificent section, the Gardens offers good swimming, plenty of orange boulders to scramble over, and free campsites.

The middle section is in the vicinity of Ansons Bay, accessed via Policemans Point or Ansons Bay's northern shore. Take your pick of 11 secluded, idyllic beaches, accessible only on foot from Ansons Bay in the north or the Gardens in the south. Nowhere along the coast are there high-rises, boardwalks, or theme parks— just the natural beauty of nearly empty beaches with white sand and rocky bays, where you are likely the only soul around for miles (not counting the wallabies, Forester kangaroos, or yellow-tailed black cockatoos, of course).

Mount William National Park is the third section of the Bay of Fires, and runs along the bay's northern edge and encompasses part of it. Remote and lonely, it was declared a national park in 1973 to protect the dwindling population of Forester kangaroos. Today, sightings of the large, agile marsupials are virtually guaranteed at dawn or dusk in open grassy areas along Forester Kangaroo Drive. An easy 1.5-hour out-and-back walk to the top of Mount William affords fabulous coast and inland views.

The beauty isn't all terrestrial, either—in the clear waters of the bay, snorkelers and divers discover a spectacular underwater garden of colorful sponges and corals, prowled by bevies of interesting, tropical fish including weedy sea dragons with waving, leaflike appendages, and rock lobsters, which lack claws and resort to a series of undignified screeching noises to keep predators away.

Waves have smoothed the boulders along the coast at Mount William National Park, on the northern end of the Bay of Fires.

▶ TRAVELWISE

• **HOW TO VISIT** The Bay of Fires extends more than 20 miles (32 km) from Binalong Bay in the south to Eddystone Point in the north. St. Helens is the region's largest town, just a few miles from Binalong Bay. The guided, four-day Bay of Fires Lodge Walk offered October to May traverses much of the bay's length (bayoffires.com.au).

• **PLANNING** The Tourism Tasmania website has travel info (discover tasmania.com.au); the Tasmania Parks and Wildlife site has info on conservation areas, including Bay of Fires (parks.tas.gov.au).

• **HOW TO STAY** The best bases are the towns of St. Helens or Binalong Bay. You have your pick of free primitive campsites in the south and middle sections of the bay.

PICTURE PERFECT

Tasmania's Wielangta State Forest harbors the world's tallest flowering tree, the *Eucalyptus regnans,* which can grow over 295 feet (90 m) tall. Photographer Bill Hatcher climbed a dozen trees to document a team of scientists collecting data on this forest of giants. "This particular tree was unique for its complicated branching," he says. "I tried to capture it by looking straight down the tree trunk as the biologist, Jim Spickler, climbed the rope." Spickler was 160 feet (48 m) above the forest floor—Hatcher 20 feet (6 m) above that.

IMAGE BY BILL HATCHER
National Geographic photographer

Weddell Sea

The word "sea" summons the wrong visual: For most of the year, the Weddell Sea is more ice than water. Even in the summer months, this southernmost part of the Southern Ocean remains covered by a massive ice shelf, and huge icebergs drift into the northwestern edge of the sea, dubbed Iceberg Alley. The ice glows blue—a sign of old, densely compacted glacial ice.

Nineteenth-century British explorer James Weddell discovered the Weddell Sea in 1823 when he happened upon an unusually open route through the ice from the South Orkney Islands. Better known than his expedition was a later, less successful one—Ernest Shackleton's. In 1914, his ship, the *Endurance*, was trapped and crushed by pack ice in the Weddell Sea, leaving the crew adrift for months. They finally reached land at Elephant Island, north of the Weddell Sea, from which every member of the crew was eventually rescued. This story of survival is a lure for some who want to witness the solitude of the sea and the crushing, shifting power of vast sheets of ice.

Anyone who plans a visit to the Weddell Sea today must share Weddell's and Shackleton's spirit of adventure. A voyage to the Antarctic Circle involves passage from the tip of South America across the notoriously stormy Drake Passage. This can be done by air, but most visitors do it by ship. There's no outward sign when your ship ventures below the significant 66° 33' S, but the crew may break out champagne: You've crossed the Antarctic Circle!

An enormous blue-white glacier looms over a tour boat in the Erebus and Terror Gulf (opposite) off the northeast coast of the Antarctic Peninsula. Humpback, minke, and killer whales all live in these southern waters (above).

Waddling exuberantly across pack ice, an Adélie penguin traverses the frozen blue-and-white landscape of Active Sound.

REWIND EXPEDITION TO THE SOUTH POLE

This photo by Herbert Ponting—along with 15 others—ran in a 1924 *National Geographic* magazine story about exploration. Ponting was the photographer who accompanied Robert Falcon Scott's doomed British Antarctic expedition in 1912. In the 1920s, not even National Geographic yet had Antarctic photography that came close to the power of Ponting's from that trip. That he survived the expedition at all (Scott and the rest of his party perished) was thanks to his middle age. He was not deemed fit enough to make the journey all the way to the South Pole, so he stayed behind at base camp when the rest of the expedition set out in 1911.

The caption for this photo, of a dog team dwarfed by a massive hunk of ice, best sums up the awesome, inhospitable landscape of Antarctica: "It has been estimated that one of the icebergs encountered by the last Scott expedition was large enough to have carried on its back the entire city of London and all its suburbs."

For many, simply watching from the bridge of the ship as it navigates the ice is a wonder. The Weddell Sea is famed for its icebergs. Some are vast white slabs with sheer faces and blocky heights; others have been beaten by the elements into smooth, tortuous forms, and are weirdly alight with that blue cast. The ships that escort visitors—icebreakers—are decidedly better equipped for the conditions than was the *Endurance*. These modern ships move through the water deftly and deliberately—forward, back, side to side, slowly, then quickly—looking for the next opening in the ice.

Tuxedoed emperor penguins, the largest and most majestic of the endearing flightless birds, are usually at the top of any Antarctic traveler's list. The continent is home to more than a half million emperor penguins, though their colonies are not easily accessible to visitors. Air temperatures at the South Pole can drop to minus 40°F (-40°C), and winds gust to 200 miles an hour (322 kph) in the winter, but the birds are well adapted to the harsh conditions.

When the ice begins to melt in the spring, some expedition ships try for Snow Hill Island in the Weddell Sea. It's the northernmost emperor penguin rookery, home to some 4,000 breeding pairs and, by November, thousands of downy white chicks. The colony is a stunning sight for those who make it all the way to the rookery—but many do not. The ice patterns need to be just right for a ship to get close enough to the island to fly passengers to land via helicopter.

An ice-breaking ship ferrying eager tourists approaches
a stretch of smooth first-year ice on the Weddell Sea.

From their ships' deck, visitors may also spot humpback, minke, and killer whales and several different types of seals, including the Weddell seal, which calls out with high-pitched rhythmic trills and sharp whistles one might mistake for dance club electronica. Bird-watchers also keep their eyes peeled for the storied albatross, made famous as a symbol of seafaring superstition and dread by Samuel Taylor Coleridge's poem *The Rime of the Ancient Mariner*. The formidable bird can live 50 years, grow wings that span 11 feet (3.4 m), and ride the ocean winds for hours without ever once flapping them.

TRAVELWISE

• **HOW TO VISIT** To explore the Weddell Sea, you must book passage aboard an icebreaker or ice-strengthened ship. Some outfitters offer air/sea combination packages. Expeditions only set out in the warmer months—typically late October through late March.

• **PLANNING** The International Association of Antarctica Tour Operators has resources for those planning a visit to the Antarctic Circle, and a list of tour operators *(iaato.org)*. Lindblad Expeditions/National Geographic also offer a "Journey to Antarctica" tour *(expeditions.com)*.

• **HOW TO STAY** Most visitors call their expedition ships home.

PICTURE PERFECT

"South Georgia Island is one of the wildest, most remote places on the planet," says photographer Frans Lanting, who was part of a rare circumnavigation of the island by private yacht. "This photo was taken in late afternoon with dreary weather, low clouds, and temperatures around freezing." He had to climb steep cliffs to get close to this colony of nesting black-browed albatrosses. "They may never have seen a human being up close before," he says.

IMAGE BY FRANS LANTING
National Geographic photographer

INDEX

Boldface indicates illustrations.

ILLUSTRATIONS CREDITS

Front cover, © Rick Sammon/500px Prime; back cover (LO), Kenneth Garrett/National Geographic Creative; Back Cover (UP LE), Joe Mamer/age fotostock/Robert Harding World Imagery; Back Cover (UP CTR LE), Matthieu Paley; Back Cover (UP CTR RT), Dragos Cosmin photos/Getty Images; Back Cover (UP RT), David Doubilet; 1, Danita Delimont/Getty Images; 2-3, Gordon Wiltsie/National Geographic Creative; 4-5, Stephen Alvarez/National Geographic Creative; 6, Hal Beral/VWPics/Redux; 8-9, Design Pics Inc/Alamy; 10-11, Frieder Blickle/laif/Redux; 12-13, Joe Mamer/age fotostock/Robert Harding World Imagery; 14, Nick Norman/National Geographic Creative; 15, Patricio Robles Gil/NPL/Minden Pictures; 16-17, Hermann Erber/LOOK-foto/Getty Images;

18-19, Patricio Robles Gil/NPL/Minden Pictures; 19, Amos Burg; 20-21, Gordon Wiltsie/National Geographic Creative; 22, First Light/Robert Harding World Imagery; 23, Heeb/laif/Redux Pictures; 24, Tibor Bognár/age fotostock; 25, Ashley Cooper/Robert Harding World Imagery; 26, Ed Darack/Getty Images; 27, Greg Vaughn/Alamy; 28, Douglas Peebles/Robert Harding World Imagery; 28-9, David Fleetham/VWPics/Redux Pictures; 30, Fotofeeling/Westend61/Corbis; 31, Randy Harris/Redux Pictures; 32-3, Julia Knop/laif/Redux Pictures; 34, B. Anthony Stewart/National Geographic Creative; 34-5, Andrew Kennelly/Getty Images; 36-7, Raul Touzon/National Geographic Creative; 38, Andreas Strauss/LOOK/Robert Harding World Imagery; 39, Tim Fitzharris/Minden Pictures; 40, Christian Heeb/laif/Redux Pictures; 41, Michael Runkel/Robert Harding World Imagery; 42,